I0569323

Butterflies and Cramps

Marsha Hunt

Dedication

For my beautiful children including my grandchildren and in memory of my fabulous friend , Diana . Inspiring the creation of this book to my sister Kathy, my Nana (deceased 1969) at a young age in search of fullfillment . Through the roller coaster of life , being a proud mother and caring friend to all those who have crossed my rocky path. There will never be anymore love in my heart than l hold for my children and grandchildren.

Acknowledgment

With love and respect l acknowledge those friends who have given support and input towards this book . Thank you Diana (deceased 2024) , Hazel , Pauline, Melissa, Amanda and Jill for the many years of friendship, encouragement and inspiration. Many more nursing friends such as Anne Marie, Julie, Susan and so many others who have empowered me to write the most cathartic and soul searching book and reaching my goals in life. I could never be me without you.

Contents

Chapter 1:
The little red haired girl

The earliest I can recall is about the age of two. I can just remember being in a house with a boy older than me. We used to play together in the house. Unfortunately, I remember vividly being in the back of a van, a red one, crying quietly to myself and his older boy with me. We were scared of the dark and there seemed a lot of shovels in the back with us. Two men were talking just outside the rear of the van, I could hear them, then everything went black. It wasn't until many years later that I learned it was my biological father and his friend Nancarrow who had taken my brother and I from Adelaide to Port Augusta in this van. We had been taken from our mother and South Australian Police were looking for us. None of that knowledge I recalled thankfully.

At the age of eighteen months or so I can remember being inside a large building, which turned out to be a hospital in Melbourne. My mother had taken me to visit a little red haired girl who had an operation. I could still see this room in my head today. I was up high and could see out the window. Years later my mother explained that she was holding me in her arms and that's how I could see out the window. The girl with the red hair was named Kathy. She was just lying on the bed, which looked like a large cot. From

1

memory she had surgery to her leg. This girl smiled at me, she told me her leg was sore. She never cried, although she must have been in pain. I only recall the three of us in that hospital room, my mum, the little red-haired girl, and myself.

Around the age of four we had a German Shepherd dog named Tuppence. In actual fact Tuppence was given to my older brother, Terry, but we all loved her and was the most loyal and protector of all of us in the family. The house we lived in at the time was a sunny open house and think it was near the beach. Eventually we moved house for some unknown reason, we moved a lot. I attended many schools which I hated. Not being able to retain friends or at least keep special mates was hard on me growing up. However, in general I was happy and enjoyed my childhood. My brother Terry and I would run down to the local beach with Tuppence in tow. Such great memories indeed. One time I was running up and down the riverbank chasing Tuppence. I slipped, fell in the river and it was only the fact that my dad grabbed my long blonde hair and saved me! My parents told me that I didn't speak for two hours! The quietest I had ever been.

I had spent a few years with my grandmother, my mum and I visited her often. Nana was absolutely wonderful to me. Nana had the biggest cat I had ever seen! I always wanted to have a fat cat like that, but I never did get one that big. My grandparents lived in a lovely country town in Victoria, Wangaratta. At one point, I am sure they lived in Sunshine, Victoria. Mavis was my mothers' sister, such a beautiful aunt. The beauty of my mother and auntie Mavis was amazing. Absolute stunners, both had jet black hair with slender figures. Hoping to be like them when I grew up, unfortunately I was the skinny one with blonde hair and blue eyes, unlike their dark eyes. Mavis married a German guy, and they ended up having three boys. At one point mum would have them stay over for weeks at a time and they were absolute devils! We all loved them anyway.

We moved once again and the most pleasurable memory at this time was spending days at my dads' Warehouse. Mum was occupied with a new baby; he was so cute with beautiful blonde hair similar to mine but was curly. I loved him so much and spent many hours playing with him. Now, back to the Warehouse, there were many boxes and cartons and my favourite biscuits were Honey Jumbles. Strange how the packets would break open while I was there helping dad. He had distinctly told me that all cartons were counted for deliveries but he couldn't sell the broken packets. It puzzled dad how many Honey Jumbles were broken on the days I was there. The were many boxes and crates of tinned food, fruit and jars that didn't get 'accidently' broken. From memory I only damaged a few, it was the most enjoyable time indeed.

Aunt Rosemary, dads sister, was so good to me. Almost every weekend and most school holidays invited me to her place in North Glenelg, SA. My two cousins, Gavin and Brent, treated me like one of the family and aunty Rosemary took us all to the big Adelaide shopping centers. Memories of having my hair curled every time I visited and riding the push bikes around Glenelg. As I was never allowed to own a bicycle due to traffic in the 60's, makes me laugh these days, however my cousins never had an issue with me riding their bikes! None of us got hit or fell off the bikes and I never told my mum or dad about the bikes either. Many happy memories of times spent at my aunts' house the good times we shared are still in my heart. My own children have wonderful memories of her house and gatherings we've enjoyed over the years. The eldest sister of my dad, aunty Pat, was not so good hearted to me during my childhood. That is from my perspective only as I wouldn't want to create any ill feelings amongst any surviving family members. Aunt Patty had two daughters and one son. Two of these cousins were great to play with as youngsters. Calculating one wasn't so much.

When we used to play outside in their yard they used to pick on me. Vividly recalling the swing which was on a slope in the yard way up in the Adelaide Hills. Every single time it was my turn to go on the swing the girls would push me as high and fast as they could. It was scary to be going that fast and overlooking a mountain sloping downwards. Each time my knuckles were white from grasping on so tight to prevent falling off and crashing down the hill. Francine and Mary laughed and pushed me higher. Truly I believe this began my fear of heights later in life. One Christmas the two girls and I were on the veranda painting Christmas Cards which was fun at the time, we were about 8, 9 & 10 years of age. As per usual I was the middle one. At the end of the activity we asked aunty Pat to choose the best one. Aunty Pat said Francine was the best as she had a flair, then I heard my aunt say to another adult in the room,

"She's not really one of us anyway, she's not a Pope". These words I just couldn't comprehend what she meant by that remark until many years later. To this day I still feel awkward in discussing her or her family. She hurt me deeply. I told my dad which consequently created a rather intensive family argument between my parents, my grandparents and my aunt. I don't remember her saying anything like that again but I did get along with cousins Mary and Andrew.

There was a weekend when I had to stay at aunt Pat's and she sent her two girls and myself to stay at her friend's place. A German couple or perhaps Dutch who lived in a very quaint house on the beach. The front yard was full of flowers and in the back yard had an old shed with a double bed, a sink which had a dripping tap. Us girls had to sleep in that shed! It was situated right on the sandy beach. It was creepy inside and the dripping tap went on all night. Sharing this bed was not fun, worse ever sleep, we could hear the waves crashing on the beach. Each time one of us rolled over, one would fall out of the bed. This continued all night, rolling, falling, back in bed, and so on! In the morning the German lady woke us up to come eat breakfast. She was a large woman with whitish grey hair, a smile on her round face and legs like tree trunks. She seemed kinder than the rather portly man. He was helping put dishes and food on the table different types of cheeses, sausages and other meats that we didn't know what they were. I noticed the man had one of his fat fingers missing! Whispering to my cousins, alerting them to the missing finger, naturally none of us ate any sausages. Not long after breakfast aunt Pat came to pick us up, I was so glad to see her and take me home to my parents.

We had moved a few more times and landed in Interstate, NSW. We also had a new baby. I had changed schools several times and managed to make new friends. We were living in a big house near the beach. The great thing about this house was our backyard met my nana's backyard! I thought this is the best house ever. My Primary Private school was right across the road from my nana, pop and aunt Kathy. The little red haired girl had grown up and was going to high school. She was so good to me and so was my nana. I went to Sunday School every Sunday, imagine that! Tuppence the German Shepherd was still around and loved the beach walks with us. At some point, my little brother stayed at my mum's friend's place and I stayed at my nana's it was so much fun. I was able to hang out with the girl with the red hair and nana. One day after school I went straight to nana's house and had a big surprise waiting for me. In the lounge room, my mum was sitting down and there was a small bundle in her arms. It was a dark haired baby girl! Everyone was making a fuss, especially my dad.

My brother, Terry, was working, in fact I don't recall him going to school, he must have but just don't remember him doing anything but working. Back in those days in the early 1960's he delivered ice, big blocks of ice to people to keep food cold and fresh. Now that makes me feel old today. It was an essential service and just as well he may have been called up to go to the Vietnam War through conscription. Terry was about eight years older than me. Aunt Kathy was about six years older. Terry had many jobs, in fact he worked at BHP steelworks in Port Kembla NSW also at another steel place at Unanderra NSW. He retired at age 38, very young, and was married with a son Matthew and three step sons. I used to babysit them all, they were all good kids for me. Matthew and I still keep in touch, he is an amazing Firefighter in NSW. He is married to a nurse and she is a wonderful young lady, and they had three wonderful children. Unfortunately, both of his parents are now deceased. In 2017 I arranged to have a family reunion in Sydney. My sister Kathy, brother Tom and my partner at the time were there along with Sandra, Matthew's mother. Fiona who is an amazing cook had made some baked goods including cupcakes and fancy biscuits. Lots of photos taken and memories made to cherish.

The family enjoy these get together gatherings but sadly each time we have one there is always one person missing. It makes you so lucky to have those family members in your life. Makes you appreciate what you have in your life at that moment in time. During Covid 19 from 2020 to 2023 we lost some very precious family members. Lovingly mentioning a few; Sandra Pope, Kerrie Pope Douglas Bruce and Aunty Gwen. The hardest thing was not being able to attend due to Covid 19 virus, unable to travel interstate and limited numbers of attendees permitted by Government Health. However, I am sure the families understood. We as a family have lost some major members in our lives. It used to be us, my generation, losing grandparents and great grandparents that we all grew up knowing our cousins. I personally feel sad that my own grandchildren either don't know their cousins or spend quality time with them as my generation did and made wonderful memories. My own children grew up with great grandparents, grandparents, aunts and uncles and playing with cousins. My brothers' and sister's children had the same opportunities and believe it was a good upbringing. But it is so hard for me to understand why this new generation born in 1970's, 1980's and even 1990's doesn't have this connection or even the desire to connect with cousins. For many years I felt it was my fault but sitting back looking at my family, including my grandchildren, none of them have that strong sense of belonging to family. My own childhood was made better by knowing my nana and pop, on both sides of the family tree. Even step grandparents were an amazing help in my life. I would love to know how to re-join my grandchildren with their cousins. Luckily my eldest son and his cousin Matthew keep in contact via Facebook and catch up when they can. My son also has an extremely close bond with his own biological father's children, creating a special bond between themselves that I am so happy about. Their father passed away in his early 30s of a cardiac condition in the 70's. They did not do heart transplants at that time.

In 1972 I was employed at Foodland in Queen St, Warilla NSW, I had left St. Mary's College, or just didn't return in 1972. My dad had said to me,

"You either get a job or you will need to return to St. Mary's College". He was very firm about that. So I spent four weeks on the beach, sand sun and surf and catching up with friends and having a great break. Of course not forgetting the chores at home my mum made me complete. It wasn't until the very last week of the school holidays that I was offered the Foodland job. Yes, thank you! Obviously I jumped at the chance at independence. Mr. G. had offered me a job packing the shelves, packing bags for customers and later on became a check out chick with my friend Esperanza. She lived in the same street as me, Bradman Ave., she was a little older than me. One dark night with stormy clouds, lightening and a huge downpour of rain, Esperanza's boyfriend came to pick her up on his motorcycle, well the three of us rode home on it together. Talk about terrifying! Going around the corners from King St., up McCabe St., and down Bradman Ave. What a spin! I was hanging on tight to Esperanza and she was hanging on tight to her boyfriend. The rain absolutely pelted down onto our faces despite I was trying to dig my face into her back. He stopped outside my house and I quickly scrambled off, maneuvering my little legs off the bike without pulling Esperanza off with me.

It was dark, wet and cold. I thanked him and waved goodbye. Once inside my home mum saw me wet as a shag.

"I'll run you a bath, Marsh". She said looking at my shaking body. She was a good mum like that. Remembering the bath and shower water heater, there was a certain way to turn it on.... water first .... or heat switch first? I could never remember and mum used to tell us kids,

"If you don't do it right it will blow up". We were all scared to touch it.

So thanks mum for the PTSD re water heaters, not to mention the pressure cooker!

For a few years we had an outdoor toilet. The Aussie Dunny. my brother and I used to swing on the door handle, often breaking it and dad forever fixing it. Tom and I swung on the Hills Hoist clothes line too, let go and spin around get dizzy and fall over laughing our heads off. Mum had planted a passionfruit vine along the side fence where the bedrooms were. There were always plenty of passionfruit but I just wasn't a fan of the fruit, more of a banana person. Banana fritters, banana sandwiches, banana splits …. that type of thing. These days I need to watch my diet, too much sugar, too much potassium. There is always something I can't eat!

We eventually upgraded to a new indoor toilet, flushed and everything! Dad converted the outdoor dunny into a flushing one too, we felt a bit fancy as we had two flushing toilets! Luxury in the 70's. A bit like 'who's who with a flushing loo' upper class. So many great childhood memories, days on the beach, white sand under our feet. Playing with the ten pound Poems and kids from all nations. Spanish, Greek and aborigines everyone was the same as us, just kids in the neighborhood. Kids from Warilla or the 'Gong'. It was our community and we loved it, protected each other, and shared good times. As we grew older I did notice there were little 'click' groups amongst the girls, didn't noticed it so much in the boys but the girls were a finicky lot … that is my nice way of saying it. Maybe it was puberty but that was the start of the bitchiness! Perhaps the beginning of discrimination and it was not pleasant being either end. Bonfire nights were the best back in the day, we brought our firecrackers and all hung out. We would light them up, under parental supervision of course, (that's my version anyway) and let the magic happen in the night sky with colorful bursts and the deflagrate, the sound was at times quite deafening. Our squeals and laughter could still be heard by neighbors.

Before our house was built in Bradman Ave., we lived in a caravan park near the lake and I loved it, the lifestyle of freedom, beach, carefree. We had two caravans actually, I think my older brother Terry stayed in one and my parents and us younger kids in the other. We did our German Shepherd, Tuppence, under the caravan as we weren't allowed to have dogs. Would you believe it, Tuppence had a litter of puppies! So cute! No surprise we couldn't keep any of them. I have no memory of having my baby sister at the caravan park or even where my grandparents lived at that stage. I would have been about seven years old, as there are six years between Tom and me. Looking back on a few black and white Kodak photos of my little brother and I, I noticed Tuppence was in it, the fence where it joined to my nana's yard. I can safely assume that at some stage before the house being built we lived at Shellharbour. That's where my private primary school was, opposite my nana. I first saw my baby sister there at my nana's. That house I distinctly remember some dark scary times. I may have blocked it out, but believe me, there were no butterflies, mainly cramps and blankness. My nana and pop seemed to be my sanctuary and of course that red haired girl, Kathy. In due course I shall rethink the darkness at that beach house. There were other people living there.

Two children who shared a long bedroom with four beds, like a long built in veranda.

Tom was staying at mums' friend's house while she was in hospital having this baby girl, it was 1963. I was fortunate to stay at nanas. When mums friend brought little Tom back when the baby came home there was an incident! Tom was about two years old with thick curly blonde hair. When he was returned he had his hair shaved off! Just like her own two sons…. OMG I think that was the first time I ever heard my parents swear, even yell loudly at anybody. My siblings and I still talk about it! Mum was not happy however his hair grew back, but I was never the same. Eventually mum and dad forgave her and Gracie felt bad about the whole incident. She never let her babysit again though.

Moving along to age 15 and working for Mr. G. at Foodland store I not just saved money but kept tins of food under my bed in a box, like a 'Glory' box. Girls used to save up things for after marriage etc. My plan was to get out and be self-supportive. Ironically I had saved items such as teacup and saucer set, Damask linen tablecloth, lots of trinkets I had won at Bingo when mum and I used to go. Ran by the local Catholic church, in Purr Purr Ave, somewhere around there. Everyone went, everyone knew each other, the mothers, the kids, the grandparents and it was fun. Unfortunately, the relationship deteriorated between my mum and me after the age of 14. We had our disagreements but we still loved each other. My distrust of others took over my whole life. Trusting the wrong ones and not believing the others …. it just made my life so unnecessarily complicated when it didn't need to be that way. For the last fifty-five years almost to the month, it has haunted me, the black dog, the suspiciousness, the black outs and the cramps. The occasional Butterflies in my life time has truly been my lifeline that has kept me alive today. Years of hard work within relationships have chipped away at my soul. A very few people in my life have kept me from the dark. And so my story continues.

My sister Kathy known as my aunt earlier on in life, was married to my older brother's mate Doug. Even though I spent lots of time at Kathy's with her two gorgeous babies, it seemed Terry and Doug spent less time together. I've always been 'aunty' to her children and she has always been known as 'aunty Kathy' to my children including my step children. We have a unique bond of sisterhood. Through good or bad we will always play the sister card. We also did not feel we needed to explain the reason why we are like we are. We often think …. would our life be any different if our mum had kept Kathy with her? Would Mum still have married Theo? Had Kevin? Had me? Too many ifs. So we need to accept what is as it is in life. You cannot change someone else's past, saying the word sorry doesn't change it, erase it or even forget it. Over the last fifteen years I have studied and researched the brain, memory, painful memories, healing of thoughts, reactions of self and others, predictable reactions to in depth physiological neurotransmitters. Including genetic hereditary traits, chromosomes, and all that science can prove. Like two siblings with the same DNA, having the same biological parents, but having two different personalities as in children and as in adults.

At which point do they change? Were they different DNA from the start? Perhaps too much father's recessive trait or not enough of maternal recessive trait? Or is it the luck of the draw? I often wondered through my nursing carerabout Nature Vs Nurture? Within my own personal family and extended siblings there are many variables of the Nature Vs Nurture theory. In a later version I will attempt at a genetic mapping of my maternal side, starting with my maternal grandparents with the limited knowledge that I have acquired over the years…in addition to my own children and grandchildren. It has been interesting to say the least. With intentions of having my own DNA done and compare what I know and what is scientifically and biologically proven. Last Christmas my eldest grandchild, now an adult told me he had undertaken DNA testing. He had discovered and quite surprised to learn he was 1% Swedish. I knew my paternal great grandfather was born in Warsaw, Poland and he married a Swedish woman and it began there to India, Russian princess and so forth. Amazing what will show up in your gene pool. I gather it would be extremely upsetting for all those transgender people who insist they are female / male; your DNA never changes. It's not a bad thing, it's who you are, ACCEPT it and move on.

Looking back on my teen years I feel that there was a period of time where I was impulsive, over reactive and moments in high school at   St. Mary's College. There would be incidents where I would be reading something in class and it would literally disappear from the page. My eyes just could not focus on a word; the written word would not be there. Everything would be blank. I never actually found out what was causing these blackouts. Mum had already had my vision tested resulting in needing glasses, which I only wore for reading. Diagnosed with Astigmatism and short sighted. Over the years my vision was tested and three separate eye specialists would say,

"Oh I see …Mm interesting.." Of course I asked about the comment, I would be told,

"Oh nothing, just something you were born with …." to this day no one has explained it to me. Maybe DNA testing may give me an answer.

During my Christian schooling we had the fear of God put into our innocent minds. Fear of burning in Hell where the Devil resides. The nuns and priests were allowed to use a cane to harshly hit a child's outstretched fingers, palm up, six good hard whacks, scarring the fingers and minds. Settling into the Amygdala section

16

of the memory part of the brain. If only we knew then what we know now! There is still have the scar on my right hand, middle finger fifty-eight years later after a whack of the cane from a nun at Stella Maris Primary School, Shellharbour NSW. Years later I managed to get rid of the traumatic memory stored in my Amygdala by chance when I was a nursing student doing my first injection on a real patient. Alas the same nun who left me scarred, redemption, karma, revenge whatever you like to call it … I was satisfied. Sister V. remembered me in that moment. I explained to her, with my senior RN in attendance,

"I am only a trainee so this is my first injection, if I hurt YOU or leave a BRUISE, I am sorry …." Her face went pale as my face smiled.

Speaking of burning in Hell, these days more people are tending to prefer cremation to burial. Is this a sign of the times? I wonder why this is occurring. Less expensive, less room in cemeteries? Perhaps the ability to take loved one's ashes anywhere you move. More of my friends and family members are keen on this option. Most of them were baptized Catholic, but no longer practicing Catholics or are non-religious. Are we being our own idealists or revenge on all the church teachings as children? Are we joining the Devil in the fire? In the end whether being buried or cremated we are still returned to ashes. Time makes the difference. Being buried takes fifty years to decompose, hundred years or so for a skeleton to decompose, whereas cremation is turn to dust / ashes within three hours. So is it a personal matter of choice or religious beliefs? The thought of cremation makes me shutter, but when you are dead … you're dead. Not alive. No pain.

You could be with your loved ones sooner in a nice Urn of your choice. Perhaps scatter at a special place, your spirit or soul has already gone before the cremation process, so they say. Burial to me is a kinder version as I recall my dad's funeral. His burial plot was always there to visit, to talk to him, to be alone with him. My mum was buried on top of him in the same plot. Never been sure how I felt about that, maybe it's psychological as I feel there is no more private time with my dad anymore. Even vice versa, no private time with my mother. I truly believe in my heart of hearts that if mum had of been cremated, my sister Margaret would have mum's ashes in a fancy box with Sunflowers and Violets on it. I would have shared Dad's ashes with my brother Tom in an urn like a book of Philosophy or a chess set. Well I think that should be that on a heavy subject, best change the mood onto something lighter.

Chapter 2:
Nursing – The Hard Yards

The lighter part of the book, my nursing career, the good the bad and the political. I had a few starts and stops in my career, many due to ridiculous rules of an era that thankfully changed. Changed so much though the pendulum has swung a dash too far, that's just my opinion. An example like ; when I was working at St. Joseph's Hospital Auburn NSW, I got married on 2nd November, and simply due to my marriage the Matron (a nun, of course) put me on a month's night shift! That didn't sit well with me or my groom. The nuns view was to prevent a pregnancy from happening so to keep nurses working. Ha-ha, as if the only time couples had sex was between 9pm and 7am! My new spouse, Mr. A we'll say for now, will elaborate further on, was not impressed after my four week stint and made me resign! He was jealous of me nursing any male patients. Looking back, I should have seen this as a red flag. So another stoppage in my carerwith no credit given by the Nurses Board of NSW for time already studied.

Due to an extremely violent domestic situation and having no help the marriage ended with me losing a baby girl at 23 weeks pregnant. Due to a violent physical injury by my husband. Who was this man that I knew years ago as Jeff, who now turns out to be

Allan? Another red flag I didn't see. Dark times ahead and not quite ready to tell as it took too many years to recover. Cramps in the darkness, blank moments, his many attempts to electrocute me, absolutely terrifying events. So I was nurse Novotny, I actually liked the sound of that and not far off from my birth name which I discover in my mid-teens, which is another whole chapter! At least I could hold my head up high and my mum couldn't make me lie about my name or who I was. The truth is the day after I turned eighteen years of age I got married, in the Sydney Marriage Registry. This is one of those impulsive, reactive moments I mentioned earlier! Not ashamed just regretful but it is what it is …. No one is perfect! The law had changed in 1973 allowing eighteen year olds to marry without parents' consent. The only regret is losing my unborn baby girl, whom I named Hayley, after the actress Hayley Mills.

My dad met me once again at the Oak Flats railway station and took me home. Battered and bruised, four broken teeth, nervousness and depressed. It took a lot of love from my mum, dad and siblings. No judgmental behavior from anyone. It had been a terrible experience and finally promised myself that no one would ever beat me like that again. At that point in my life that was the worst thing a man could do to me. There were absolutely scary situations that occurred that I would have preferred a beating! At this point it is very hard to write or talk about. Such as being locked in a wardrobe, for hours, had a light globe inserted with threats of smashing it to cause injury, pulling me by the hair to a kitchen sink full of water trying to electrocute me with a frypan electrical cord. one end plugged into power point and other end immersed in the water! There were worse situations I endured from this man. I thank my mother for her understanding of my terror. She knew the horror and the pain.

After a few months of dental work, Valium to settle my nerves and shakes and with my dad's help with getting me an interview at Shoalhaven Memorial Hospital, I was recovering. Dad knew the Matron and thank goodness wasn't a nun. However, I had to wait once again for the Nurse's Board of NSW for approval. Again not giving me any credit for any past training, exam results, skills acquired by either Victor Harbor South Coast Hospital SA or St. Joseph's hospital NSW. This seemed so unfair to me, but at least the Board were considering letting me start over, I felt I would be ahead of the other students with previous skills attained. As per usual the Matron agreed to allow me to begin working as a Trainee Nurse's Aide until we heard back from the Board. I was very thankful as Matron knew of my former marriage situation and discreetly kept it to herself.

Nurse Novotny was back on track, a new start and the good news eventually came from the Nurses Board NSW. Yes! I was approved but with an added note of my many breaks in training and

"The Board views this seriously and will look carefully at any further breaks in training". Due to this I was given a 12 month Registered Nurse's Aide enrolment, RNA, which equaled to today's version of Enrolled General Nurse. I was pleased enough with that to pursue my nursing career. Thinking of my nana Crosbie and dedication to helping others. I could continue to help patients with compassion and passion for learning as many skills as I could. Working in surgical wards was so interesting as I could actually see tissues, cells growing to complete and repair wounds from surgical incisions, trauma causing lacerations. There was the fascination from large abdominal surgeries to minute scar tissues that join and heal over. It was like magic! Aseptic technique was my forte. No spreading germs, no inflammation and no sepsis.

Working in medical wards was probably the hardest for me at this early stage of my career. Chest infections, phlegm, pneumonia, infectious wounds and TB. During the 70's there seemed many patients with diabetes with gangrene and amputations. Not so much mental illness like today's society, however saying that, in early 1974 I was on night shift in the casualty department when I received a call from a woman saying her son had problems breathing. So I immediately advised to bring him into the casualty. I notified the RN working with me and she advised the duty doctor, who was asleep in the hall on a spare bed. Back in those days the hospitals used a switchboard telephone system. I hated it, was always hanging people up accidentally. We all began preparing for this child to be presented, oxygen and oxygen tent, medications all at the ready. Perhaps an acute asthma attack?

We kept looking and waiting for a car to rock up at the casualty department entrance. After an hour and no, one came, the duty doctor informs us that he has his pager on, if she arrives. The three of us came to the conclusion that the danger had dispersed and all was ok. The Registered Nurse resumed to her progress notes and I returned to the complicated switchboard. Thank goodness day shift had trained staff who knew what they were doing, and I was lucky there were not many calls at 2am. A little after 3am a lady came in with a suitcase. First thing I did was grab a pen and notebook to take down any details, when she promptly heaved the rather old, large and gritty suitcase onto my desk. I looked up at her and said,

"Can I help you?". to which she replied without any conviction or urgency,

"I called earlier my child couldn't breathe". I nodded looking towards the entrance expecting a man to be carrying in a child.

"Yes of course". The totally unexpected happened! The woman casually opened the suitcase as if presenting gift. OMG, before me was a child's body, cut up. Head swollen. I was almost immediately sick. My first response to her was,

"No wonder he can't breathe!"

23

After quickly getting the RN who was behind a curtain checking an IV on a patient,

"Please come quick". I begged her grabbing her arm. She came and went pale at the sight before her. The woman was encouraged to take a seat in an empty bay. Duty doctor was paged and the Police were called. The RN and I just stared at each other for a moment or two.

I was only eighteen, my first night shift with a second year RN, an Intern and a crazy woman who had chopped up her five year old son and put him in a suitcase! I was in shock and I had to keep it together and be professional. The Police arrived asking heaps of questions such as; how did the woman present, upset or emotional ? Any eye contact? I thought to myself never mind about her, what about me …? After answering all the questions by the Police the Matron came on duty and the morning staff were getting handover. There was one Policeman with the lady and another Policeman went to the morgue where they had taken the little boy's remains. Matron took me aside and spoke quietly and calmly to me and praised me for my professionalism. I definitely did not feel that at all. There were fierce cramps and on the verge of blanking out. On returning to the nurse's quarters I quickly fell into a deep sleep, not waking until 4pm.

After a long shower, dressed into my jeans and tee shirt I went for a walk into town to clear my head. The next few night shifts left on my roster were unaffected by drama. A few asthma attacks and a couple of chest pain patients, but nothing quite as traumatic as the lady and the suitcase. Apparently she was sent to Kenmore Psychiatric Hospital for three months only. My interests at that stage was cardiology. I could illustrate a perfect heart with all four chambers to scale and in full color. The study group, PTS, as they were known, the theory part of training, became more interesting with each subject. The prior training must have paid off and of course the human body parts had not changed! In later years when I attended university to upgrade to Registered Nurse from Enrolled Nurse there were no concessions or credit recognition in anatomy module, which surprised many of us older Enrolled nurses who had been nursing a long time. We did not hear of any new parts being discovered in 29 years, like the heart, lungs, brain, liver or kidneys. No extra ribs or organs had changed position! Yes I am being a bit sarcastic, but really? learn from scratch ?

Whilst working on the Maternity ward, the Midwife in charge, Sister L., despite the fact she never married or had a baby, she knew everything to do about pregnancy and birthing. She was very strict with the nursing staff, especially student nurses, however she was kind and understanding in a professional manner to all new mums, pregnant mums and mums in general. Sr. L. also lived in the nurses quarters, she may be a tyrant at work but she was nice to us girls (a one male nurse) in the nurses quarters, baking cakes and biscuits making the place smell of fresh baking and gave it a homely feel.

For a night out three of the nurses and I went to the pub in Nowra for Chinese tea, best meal in town. We made a habit of getting together each pay week. This particular night we overindulged in a few alcoholic drinks and a huge Chinese banquet. My favourite was sweet & sour pork, fried rice and banana fritter with ice cream. This night we tried several dishes and shared the banquet. We decided to get a taxi home instead walking. Unfortunately, we did and the taxi driver took us home to the nurse's quarters without incident on the way. Until he stopped. As Patricia stepped out of the front door the driver jumped out to open the rear passenger door for Mary to get out. I was sitting in the middle seat in the back and was trying to slide over to get to Mary's side when I felt a pain in the gut. As I was moving closer to the edge of the seat the driver went to help me. That's when it happened! I threw up over the back seat, Chinese food and brandy! What a combination. My embarrassment increased when the driver told Patricia to grab a towel out of his taxi boot. He wiped my face with it and then the seat. Am not sure how many 'I'm so sorry' I uttered. He placed the towel back into the boot and said he'd wash it later not to worry about it.

We paid the fare and ran inside. I headed straight for the shower, getting vomit out of my long tangled blonde hair. I then made a cuppa tea and went to say goodnight to the other girls who had gathered in the main lounge area. Patricia surprised me by commenting on the cab driver.

"Did you notice how he was looking at you?" I laughed out loud and replied,

"The only thing I noticed was my embarrassment at chucking up over his back seat, poor guy. Hope we don't get into his taxi again in a hurry". My tummy had definitely settled down and was feeling very sleepy. I bid them goodnight and went to my room. Once snuggled under my blankets I fell into a deep sleep. My week was about to start with more theory training, which I always looked forward to, no working nights and starting later in the morning.

One of these study nights, the taxi driver, Barrie, turned up at the nurse's quarters and rang the doorbell. One of the student nurses opened the door and let him in the foyer. When he asked to see me Patricia ran up the stairs shouting my name, almost breathless. Opening my door I almost looked for a fire!

"What's all the noise and yelling". I asked looking at the expression on her face, as if she'd found the master key to the pantry. She looked so excited and was bursting to tell me the taxi driver was downstairs and asked for me! Personally I thought he must have come back with a car cleaning bill. Quickly I changed into my favourite jeans and threw on an old tee shirt. In a flash I dragged a brush through my hair and ran downstairs. He was sitting in one of the Canadian Oak chairs in the foyer. He appeared much taller than I remembered, or at least long legged. Slight wavy blonde hair and noticed the walking socks, yes the walking socks this is one thing I shall always remember him by. When he smiled when I came downstairs, I knew then he was not there for any car cleaning bill.

"I hope you don't mind; just thought you might want to go for a coffee or drink sometime?

He stood up to meet me at the bottom of the stairs, he looked so tall, I was only five feet two inches so he must have been at least six feet tall. Admittedly I didn't notice the night we met. Too busy throwing up. We just chatted in the lounge room. I told him about my studies, how much I was enjoying it all and explained I was limited with going out times.

Barrie stated he too was limited as he was separated with two beautiful children, a boy Mark, and a girl Kylie. So we made arrangements for a casual catch up with a dinner sometime. I left it like that and as he left he surprised me with a kiss on the cheek! He was gentle and had that kindness type of aura about him. I liked him.

We had a few catch ups and rarer to have sleepovers in the nurses quarters, often we would stay at my friends' place, Gail, who lived in Bomaderry. Gail worked in the server at the hospital. It was fantastic during study weeks as it gave me weekends off. Gail was married with a two-year-old son. Sometimes I would babysit him and stayover. One night we went to a Navy pilots party somewhere near a forest, it seemed a long way from Bomaderry. Gail and I had an awesome time at this party until someone started a floor fight after way too many drinks. Gail and her husband decided it was time to go home. We literally all drove home together. Her husband was behind the steering wheel, Gail was next to him with foot on the clutch pedal, and I was in charge of the brake. I don't think anybody had control of anything, somehow we all drove home and arrived safely. Laughing and switching hands to steer the car. Am pretty sure we missed a few kangaroos on the way!

Waking up the next morning I was laying on the carpet in the lounge room. There were a few newspapers opened and laid out on top of me. Looking across the room I could see Gail curled up a few feet away, also on the floor covered with newspapers. My head was aching and could hardly recall the night before. Gail eventually woke up, got up and sleepily muttered a "Morning" to me. I decided to have a shower while Gail made us black coffee and an attempt at toast. Gail had this amazing kitchen! There was an incredible wall of spices and herbs, rows and rows of little spice containers.

Naturally she was a great cook. She knew everything that blended together to enhance the flavors of each in any dish. However not on this particular morning. It was Sunday we had the day off, I had plans to meet Barrie that afternoon. He was becoming a regular visitor. We even spoke about getting a little flat somewhere in Bomaderry, hopefully near Gail.

Barrie was soft spoken, slightly old fashioned as he was a few years older than me, which I didn't mind at all. He had a beard which I did mind, but it was him, so tolerated the beard. My mum used to say,

"Don't trust a man with a beard". She never told me why but mum used to quote lots of things like that. Barrie was gentle and kind to me, I felt safe and loved when he was around. Gail and her husband Paul liked him too. When we were looking at flats to rent I became nauseated and unfortunately once again threw up in his taxi. This time it wasn't caused through alcohol or Chinese food. A quick doctors checkup and blood test confirmed I was pregnant ! I was delighted. Barrie and I drove to Warilla to tell my parents. I recall taking my little sister to the drive in to celebrate. No idea what we saw as halfway through the movie my sister and I went to the restroom while Barrie got some refreshments. To my horror I realized I was bleeding.

I was crying so much as I was trying to explain this to my sister. I was sobbing my heart out telling Barrie. Everything went blank. I can only remember Barrie taking my sister home while I went to Wollongong hospital via ambulance. The darkness was back, there was a nurse leaning over me calling my name. Slowly opening my eyes, I saw a few people around me. A doctor? My dad? I could barely hear the doctor.

"I am sorry Mrs. Novotny, you've had a miscarriage ....." I didn't hear anything else. Wondering where Barrie was, felt confused and thought he must have gone to work, I had no idea what day it was at that point. After a D & C, I was discharged. It was an extremely quiet drive home with my dad. Mum had rung the Matron to explain without explaining that I wouldn't be available to work until tomorrow. As it was my last study week I would have to ensure I caught up on my return, which I did.

When I returned to the nurse's quarters, I just laid on my bed with hands on my abdomen, tears cascading down my cheeks, my mind recalled the sadness of losing my first baby at 23 weeks of pregnancy. It also brought back memories of the traumatic and violent incident that caused the loss. However, this pregnancy was loss through no fault of my own. Wasn't sure how I was going to tell Barrie. Would he be relieved or disappointed? Maybe I can't stay pregnant? Grabbing a tissue, I dabbed at my wet cheeks. I managed to see Barrie early the following week. We decided to rent a one-bedroom place in Bomaderry, Lynburn Ave. It was a duplex. Unfortunately, we hardly spent many nights together as my rostered shifts and his shifts only gave us two nights a week home at the same time. I would try and stay awake for him and make him a cup of tea.

Some weekends we would take his children out for the day or have a sleepover. I am not sure what the kids understanding was of me or the relationship I had with their father. Both the children were always polite when we had them. Mark was tall, about 7 years of age and definitely had his father's looks. Barrie had an oval shaped face, the beard as I've mentioned and about 95% of the time wore long socks to just below his knees with shorts and closed shoes. He was definitely not a Levi jeans and white tee shirt type of guy. More so tall, dark and handsome with serious traits, not in a negative way. Mature would be a better way to describe him. I was nineteen years old, I look back and realize I was too kind and naïve for my own good. Having convinced myself that he deserved to spend more time with his children at their bedtime and tuck them in, so they could remain with his parental flow of things. I had a lot of nursing study and exams coming up so I was fine with that.

As we only had two days in January in 1975 to actually spend any time together due to both our work schedules, I cherished the quality time we had, the plans we would make for our future. We had some amazing breakfasts together. There never was a time where I saw him angry, at anyone. He made me feel truly loved and had more quality time than quantity of time. That was absolutely enough for me at that time. I was happy. One day I felt this sore throat happening, so went to the doctors', diagnosing myself with tonsillitis and needing antibiotics. Nurses are good at that, but the worst patients. The Doctor hadn't seen me since the miscarriage and did some blood tests as I was prone to low iron levels. Two days later I went back to get the results and start antibiotics. Dr. Erwin welcomed me into the room, gesturing towards the empty chair. I searched his face to try and ascertain if there was something wrong or not. He confirmed I did have tonsillitis, but unable to give me any antibiotics. He continued to explain why,

"You are actually five to six weeks pregnant. Very early stage". He smiled and waited for my reaction. I sat back in the chair and thought … holy hell! My history with pregnancies concerned me. Would I miscarry again? I really wanted to be a mother. I voiced my concerns to the doctor. He put me on a high iron enriched diet, good rest, no lifting and definitely no stress! The stress would be hard with work, study and Barrie's long working hours…. sure no problem! At this point in my training I was working in the Maternity Ward and in the labor ward, so no real heavy lifting. Feeling absolutely ecstatic at the thought of having my own little baby. On working out dates there were only a few days that I could have conceived.

My original EDD (expected due date) was 3rd November, thinking how wonderful, perhaps have the baby on my birthday, 1st November. Happily leaving the doctor's surgery with lots of ante natal pamphlets, an overload of information on how to be healthy to grow a healthy baby. On the way home I went to Nowra Mall and selected two maternity dresses, went straight home and tried then on. Did the sideways check in the mirror, made me laugh as I patted my flat tummy and prayed this baby stays forever. I never thought that moment of contentment, joy and fulfilment would ever end. I was going to be a mother. Someone that belonged to me and I can love unconditionally. It didn't matter if it was a boy or a girl as Barrie had one of each. This will be my first born, please God don't take this child from me.

Working a day shift the next day and already tired, but wanted to wait for Barrie to come home, eager to tell him the good news. It was quite a stormy night with rain pelting down the roads, making them very dangerous around Bomaderry right through to Huskisson. I waited till 11pm but he still hadn't come home. Perhaps he had got a fare to Eden or Bateman's Bay beings no trains from Nowra – Bomaderry railway station. The weather was concerning me, there may have been an accident. I curled up on the couch with a crocheted blanket from my parent's caravan. about midnight I saw headlights in the driveway shining through the small lounge window. I jumped up to open the door, the wind and rain was pelting onto the small porch splashing into the flat. Barrie was hanging onto the beam absolutely dripping wet. He was just standing there! I hadn't realized that he had been drinking, that was definitely not like him at all. I gestured him inside as he was drenched, and it was only then that I noticed he was crying, as I watched the tears rolling from his cheeks.

Chapter 3:
The Last Farewell

I sat him down and fetched a towel to dry his face, his beard and kissed his cold wet cheeks. I had never seen him cry before. I only knew him as a soft hearted and gentle man, but never seen him drunk or so upset. After a while, probably ten minutes but seemed like hours, he calmed down enough to be coherent to tell me what was wrong.

"Are your children ok?" searching his face for a clue. I made him a cup of tea and wrapped another towel around his shoulders. Our little flat didn't have heating… hell we didn't even have a phone. It was the 70's. I wanted to cheer him up from whatever bad day he had endured, so I told him I was pregnant again and the doctor would be taking good care of me not to miscarry again. I was smiling and holding his hands so tight and hoped that would cheer him up. In fact, he went quite pale, grabbed me and hugged me so hard for so long. He kissed me on the forehead and said he was happy for me. He touched my abdomen and hugged me again. Many years later I remembered this particular night and it was a bittersweet incident as I discovered he had hidden a devastating secret from me.

By this time, it was 1.15am, both of us were so tired and we had work in the morning. We just cuddled up the couch for about twenty minutes before he uttered those words I can never forget.

"I saw my doctor today too…. actually, it was the Cardiologist …" he took a big breath and held me close to him.

"My heart is failing me; I have Cardiomyopathy…." Barrie just burst out in tears and hugged me tight again.

"He says I have approximately … two years…." OMG! It was a huge shock to me, I had no words. I burst into tears and everything went blank for me. Cramps. I couldn't breathe, couldn't speak.

Due to exhaustion we laid on top of the bed trying to process both of our news. It was a dark time for both of us. But now it's the three of us. We have this little baby trying to grow. We will always have this piece of us. Even if there's only one to care for it. There will always be love to give. The windy storm continued through the night as we fell asleep in each other's arms, only to wake to the alarm clock. We showered and got ready for work, had a cup of tea and made plans to have dinner together and discuss how we would process the situation. How could God be so cruel? Barrie was the kindest and gentle person I knew, apart from my dad and brother Terry. Making the decision not to tell anyone yet at work about the pregnancy or Barrie's prognosis, it was just too hard to bear.

It was early days yet… there was a lot to consider.

We had a pub counter tea, the ambience was setting a tone of warmth and calmness. So we began the long and deep conversation, discussing the pros and cons. we laughed, we cried we held onto each other. Driving home was unusually quiet as we were each in our own thoughts. I was hoping for some butterflies, but alas only the cramps in the darkness. How could I maintain strength and courage during this pregnancy that I wanted so much. Two years …. Approximately. How would it affect Mark and Kylie? As the next few weeks went by my uniform became tighter, my boobs were getting bigger, and definitely didn't need them any bigger! Barrie and I went on a few dates to make memories. I recall the day he drove me to see his brother, Bob. Barrie went to open my door when we both heard,

"Don't bother about getting out of the car! You're not welcome here". I felt so ashamed as I knew they did not approve of me, the homewrecker, I didn't realize Barrie was still married to Ross, separated but not divorced. I was even divorced either come to think of it. So I guess I was the homewrecker. For the first time I began to wonder if he was separated at all. To think I trusted him 100%. Many tears later the truth came out.

It was clear that the family didn't want to know me or our baby. I hit me harder than I thought it would. Barrie apologized to me and we just drove away. The picnic at Shoalhaven Heads was more fun and I was wearing my new maternity dress as jeans weren't fitting anymore. He told me how 'beautiful' I was sitting at the picnic table in my dress. The warm summer breeze flowed through my long blonde hair. Cherishing the quality times, we had together. Always in the back of my mind … limited time. We talked about our future including this precious baby who was growing well and healthy. Apart from the morning sickness and afternoon nausea, I was enjoying this pregnancy, buying little clothes, despite not knowing if it was a boy or a girl. It was becoming obviously aware that I was pregnant to the staff, especially the Matron and Sr. L. Unfortunately, hospital policy viewed that I was a liability at work whilst pregnant.

Matron has discussed this with my doctor! Without my knowledge or consent! I was so angry about that. I pleaded my case as I wasn't doing any heavy lifting, I was delivering newborns into the world! Thank goodness policies have changed over the years. So I had to leave, leave my work, my training and my pay check. Extremely upset as I only had four months to go till finishing! Oh the Nurses Board will not be happy. To add insult to injury, I will eventually lose Barrie, who has been my rock. I went to Kiama Catholic Church... have a few words to God. The Department of Social Security, now known as Centrelink, put me on 'sickness benefits' whilst pregnant. I had to learn to live on $84.00 a fortnight.

I moved out of Lynburn Ave. flat. Moved into a nicer beach front unit right on Kiama Beach in William St. Just a few houses from the Kiama Hospital where I had booked into Biralee Maternity. My niece, nephew and my sister were all born there. At the time it was the best place to go to have a baby. These days it has been turned into aged care facility. I am glad I decided not to have my baby at Shoalhaven Hospital as it turned out a better option.

Barrie saw me as much as he could, between working, his kids and hospital visits. After a heartbreaking decision, sadly I had to tell him that he should be making memories with his children, Mark and Kylie, as they deserved that and they loved their daddy. Considering our baby hadn't been born yet. We agreed to reassess the situation after the baby was born. Thinking of baby names together, if a girl perhaps Patricia (Trish) or Natalie. If a boy Joshua or Bradley. Nothing was set in stone. I liked the name Bradley as I grew up in Bradman Ave., and a character on a soap opera show was Brad. Either way not to worry as I was only just over three months pregnant. How wonderful to pass the first trimester, and so proud of my growing belly. My new EDD was 12th November. So more time with me, safe and sound. I missed Barrie so much and I just assume he went back home to Ross. He wanted to stay with me at Kiama a couple days a week. But unfortunately that wouldn't work for me, I had always been and still am an ' All or nothing' type of person. Especially where my heart is concerned, plus I have this baby to think of now. I swear every time Barrie had appointments at St. Vincent's Hospital the baby would kick me!

I felt a new respect for his wife, who I thought was his ex-wife, as she would have two beautiful children to care for alone. I believed my family would support me. I would get messages from Barrie via my parent's phone, updates on his medical condition, I believed all was going well. Once I settled into my beach unit at Kiama I got the train to Sydney to visit an old friend, Colleen. She had literally saved my life in1974, from a violent domestic situation, from Mr. A. Apparently Colleen had separated herself but not in the same situation. One of her friend's brother, Shane, was visiting at the time. Shane and I hit it off straight away, little did I know this chance meeting would change my life and that of my unborn baby forever.

I explained to Colleen about my pregnancy and Barrie with his prognosis with Cardiomyopathy and no chance of a heart transplant. The first heart transplant wasn't done until 24th February 1984 on a 39 yr. old performed by Dr. Victor Chan.

"Professor K. Dwyer. Faculty of Health. Deakin University". So unfortunately too late for Barrie. Colleen was so supportive and even Shane offered to drive me home to Kiama. I thought holy hell we've only just met! I thanked him and said I was used to the old red rattler from Sydney to Wollongong line. Just to note it was only a couple of stops past my old favourite, Oak Flats Station.

I loved my sunny unit in Kiama, the beach, the surf and relaxed lifestyle. One day my mum picked me up to go to the Catholic Church in Kiama, I was about 4 or 5 months pregnant. The deal was I needed to go to confession to be a sponsor for my little sister's confirmation. A Catholic ritual we all had to go through. Mum drops me off and waves goodbye like the Queen of England, saying she'll be back soon. Two hours later, whilst I was sitting on the steps of the church for ages, mum finally shows up.

"What took you so long?" I wasn't impressed at all hanging around for nearly two hours.

With an evil laugh, mum said "I thought you'd be there confessing your sins for ages!"

On one of those rare moments where Barrie and I had a catch up at our mutual friends who lived in Nowra South on a farm, I could see the anguish in his eyes. He never complained to me of anything, but he wanted to be there for me and our baby. He would ask if I needed anything.

"I need you and our baby needs you, but your children need you more". In my heart I felt that perhaps in time Mark and Kylie could share him at some point. But was I willing to share him Ross? Maybe when they grew older, would they remember me and accept their sister or brother? I became more depressed after being with Barrie for a few hours, not just knowing time is running out for him and how he must be feeling about it too. But not knowing if this baby will be accepted and recognized as a Walker like Mark and Kylie. Barrie and I both cried and our friend Donna hugged us both.

One Saturday there was a knock at my door and was so surprised to see Shane standing there with a smile on his face. He really shocked me, but also pleasantly surprised to see him. He was like a breath of fresh air. Shane did have a nice body, dressed in his blue jeans and tee shirt! I could feel the stare of his blue eyes fixed on mine. His mouth was perfect and when he kissed me hello, I knew then it was perfect. gesturing him inside and offered him a coffee. He replied "2SM", quick as a flash I looked at him and he enlightened me as he sat on the couch.

"Two sugars and milk". I smiled and nodded. We chatted for hours about his life, my life even opened up to him about my previous marriage to Allan, including the violence I endured and the loss of my baby daughter, Hayley at 23 weeks pregnant.

"I am trying to keep de stressed, calm and content during this pregnancy". I got up to put the kettle on again when Shane came up behind me and gave me a hug. He turned me around and kissed me.

The next morning, I woke to the aroma of coffee and toasted cheese, for two. I didn't really know what to say. Thank you came to mind, but didn't come out of my mouth. Shane sat on the edge of the bed and leaned over to grab his coffee mug. I smiled and said,

"So you like toasted cheese sandwiches?" nodding toward the two thick freshly toasted sandwiches.

"Only after good sex!" He smirked a very cheeky grin. We both burst out laughing. It felt like we had known each other for years. That was the beginning of a new era. More of a rollercoaster of life, but I have never regretted meeting Shane. He had invited me to go with him to meet his mate who was in hospital, I think from memory it was a knee operation …. not 100% on that. So I showered and off we went to the Richmond RAAF Base. It was May 1975 and a very long drive from Kiama to Richmond but we chattered heaps on the way. Shane was very easy to talk to and it certainly took my mind off Barrie and his hospital visits. It was around this time that it came to my attention via my dad that I would need to legally change my name. As I was still married to Allan and my name still Novotny, so legally I couldn't register this child as Novotny as it wasn't his child. I changed my name about 15th May 1975 through a lawyer in Wollongong, to Marsha Walker. At least this baby will have his or her name as birth right.

The day Shane took me to visit his mate, Glenn, in the RAAF hospital was quite interesting. Enjoying the thrill of being on the RAAF base, hearing the roar of the planes it was breathtaking and exciting just to be that close to the Hercules aircrafts! I had wanted to join the RAAF, well the WRAAF. The smell of the fuel made me tingle, gave me butterflies. As we walked through the security gates and RAAF personal, I thought back to when I was fifteen years old with a strong desire to become an airhostess, aircrew as known today. My attempt to enlist in the RAAF then but too young, to join as an air hostess I was too short. According to criteria back then you had to be five foot five inches. Unfortunately I was only five foot two inches! No matter how many times my friends tried to pull my legs, I couldn't get any taller.

My thoughts were interrupted by the sight before me. A young man, tall, dark hair and definitely handsome, with deep brown eyes in shorts, lying on top of the hospital bed. Shane introduced me to his mate, Glenn. I could hardly speak! I just stood there at the side of the bed, taking it all in.

"Hi I'm Marsha". Was all I could finally utter. He looked exactly like a young Elvis Presley. Glenn smiled and just said,

"Hi." Shane and Glenn were chattering amongst themselves about cars, other mates and whatever. I observed Glenn's mouth moving as he talked, his expressions and to my surprise the length of his legs. He gave me butterflies for sure. Don't recall how long we were there, obviously not long enough. Shane and I said goodbye and drove back to Kiama. Shane stayed long enough for a '2SM' before he drove back to Revesby as he had work the next morning.

Enjoying the sleep in the next day, stretching out and hoping not to get any morning sickness. After a hot soapy shower, I managed to keep down a weak cup of tea with half a slice of toast before going on my usual morning walk along the beach. I had no shoes on as I loved the feeling of the sand under my feet. As I strolled along the beach thoughts came to mind about the past weekend with Shane. He seemed quite smitten with me. I laid on the beach on my back seeing and feeling my growing baby bump. Closing my eyes feeling the sunshine on my legs, loving the warmth and my baby moving around. What an amazing sensation to know my baby has moving and growing so well. I used to have naps on the beach. Kiama was a really scenic touristic town with lots of attractions like the Blow Hole. The Lighthouse was established in 1887. Back in the 1920's the Principal Keepers House was apparently destroyed by vandals. Interestingly there is no access to the Lighthouse itself. (Tourism@kiama.com.au)

Barrie hadn't contacted me for a while and I assumed he had been in and out of hospital, also assuming he had returned to his former, or estranged wife to ensure his children, Mark and Kylie, were close during this time. I kept in contact with my friends, Donna and Helmut in South Nowra. They knew about Shane and how our friendship was becoming closer. My mum really liked Shane, out of the relationships encountered, mum always favored Shane. She accepted all his friends. Shane's parents were decent people and I daresay they would have tried to talk him out of being involved with an older woman, not yet divorced having a baby to a married man with two children! Seeing it written down in words it was a lot. However, that is what Shane wanted to do for me and this soon to be born baby. He truly loved me and this child meant so much to him, even though he was only 18 years old. Shane had only just started his apprenticeship as a cabinetmaker. I owed him so much.

Most weekends were spent with Shane and his mates. Derek was an apprentice mechanic; Glenn the RAAF guy was an aircraft fitter. There were also Peter, Stevie and the brothers Bob and Bill. There were a few more but just recall them. We were like a gang, always hanging out. Towards the last trimester we tended to stay close to home. I had moved into my parent's caravan in the driveway of our home in Bradman Ave., Warilla. We had some hilarious times at my parent's place. Mum got on well with Shane and especially his mates Derek and Stevie. One night we dressed Stevie up in 'drag' and made him walk down the main street of Kiama. We all had such a laugh, even mum. Derek and Shane went fishing this particular Sunday afternoon on the 23rd November 1975 while I stayed in the caravan playing cards with my sister when suddenly had this lower back pain.

I was sitting opposite her cross legged and said.

"I can't move". Margaret looked at me and then the cards ...

"Yes you can, put the ten on the Jack"! She laughed pointing to the sets of cards laid out.

I explained I was physically in pain and couldn't move off the bed. She ran into the house to tell mum who quickly came, got me onto her bed and began massaging my belly. Contractions had started and I got scared. there were no mobile phones back then, so no way to contact Shane or Derek who were still out fishing somewhere. The week prior I had experienced some pains but the hospital sent me home saying it was just ' Braxton Hicks, false labor. Mum ran me a hot bath, made me drink some horrible tasting crap drink in orange juice. The taste almost made me throw up. Back on mum's bed she began massaging my belly and lower back with olive oil. This was to prevent 'stretch marks' or so she believed. It actually worked!

So here I am in labor with my first full term baby, unable to contact Shane or Barrie and mum hovering over me. She brought in these very old vintage type photo albums looking about 100 years old, showing pictures of my grandparents and great grandparents. There were some of my great grandmother and fascinating photos of relatives I had never met. A photo came to my attention that I thought I had recognized. Mum says no I hadn't met her, even mum hadn't met her. Curious I asked more questions as I was sure I had seen her before.

"She was my grandmother, Caroline Carpenter and she died before I was even born!" first time I saw a sadness upon mum's face. I still maintained I had seen her. Yes! I remembered. While I was staying at my nana's house in Wangaratta my little sister and I were sleeping on the couch in the lounge room. It folded into a bed. When the lights were off I could see a shadow in the corner of the window on the curtains. It was in the shape of a lady, wearing beautiful Victorian gown, an oval face and her hair up in a bun. It was my great grandmother! Caroline Carpenter. She had died in 1906 and was buried at Bairnsdale Victoria. Incidentally I went there in 2011 to find my grandparents, Martin Carpenter and Caroline Carpenter, but most of the graves only had markers and I couldn't find them. It was a 40 degree sweltering hot day and I had wandered around that cemetery for hours. Sadly, I saw so many very young children and babies buried along with adults who the average age were in their 50's and the children were averaged at 2 years of age. Feeling quite emotional already not finding Caroline's grave, but the overwhelming grief for these children. Mum concluded that my great grandmother was watching over me and we accepted this explanation I took the photo for a keepsake. I still have it in my possession. My second eldest granddaughter, Imogen, reminds me so much of her with same oval face.

Mum decided it would be a fantastic idea to take me to her friend's place, as her husband had a semi-trailer and the ride would shake this baby up. Oh yeah! Just what I needed a wild ride in a truck around some winding roads with pot holes in the darkness. I honestly thought I was going to give birth right there in the cabin of the truck! Luckily I had already been to the toilet. Finally, back at Mrs. Monahan's house and out of her husband's truck, mum had another brilliant idea. She decided to walk me up the main road, which was called Lake Illawarra Road, it may have been Lakes Entrance Road. It has been a while, anyway the whole area is now a complete concrete freeway of confusion. Mum said so seriously "We're not going to the hospital until you have contractions every second house". It was awful, it was cold, feeling like I would collapse at any moment and have my baby on the street! One of mum's friends Gracie, the one who shaved my little brother's head, visited me just a week prior to all this happening. She claimed to be a psychic, more likely a psycho, however she held her hands over my abdomen and declared my baby was a boy and date of birth being 24th November. Well we all thought she was a bit crazy. I kept saying this baby is overdue. Of course there were days in the final weeks that I felt I was going to be pregnant forever! I could hardly see over my belly, and one time on the way to the GP surgery for a checkup I fell over and scraped my knee. The GP laughed when I wanted the baby checked post my tumble,

"You are so round your baby would not have been injured"! I was not impressed.

The contractions were coming more often and felt stronger making it difficult to walk. Mum thought my timings were right (oh thanks !) so her friend helped bundle me into the backseat and off we went to Kiama hospital, straight to Birilee maternity unit. The road was very winding and steep at the best of times, but at 6.30am was still dark and cold and I didn't think I would make it at all. Hands tightly holding onto my belly as if it was crystal. We arrived, the Midwife admitted me and without warning or asking for my consent either, gave me an enema. It was futile explaining I had drunk Castrol oil in orange juice in a hot bath and could absolutely guarantee her that I had nothing left in the tank. She did it anyway. Being totally exhausted from the walking and definitely scared being my first labor. I wondered if mum or dad had contacted Barrie. Shane would have been at work by this time. The time was 7am and the Midwives and nurses were having handover. I had been placed in the labor room as apparently my screams were too noisy and frightening the other mums to be !

Chapter 4:
My Baby Boy !

Frantically pressing the nurses' bell beside, me, the back pain was the worse and there was no real position that was comfortable. The dayshift Midwife popped her head in and told me they had sent my mother home, Dr Schumacher will be in at 9am and you will probably get sent home. I saw her name badge, 'Melanie', I screamed out.

"I am going to have this baby NOW or going to shit the bed!" she ran to get another nurse who ran in and yelled,

"OMG, I am not scrubbed up yet!" as she was checking me out, Melanie told me to push,

I was so exhausted and yelled back,

"I can't" and just at that moment I heard,

"That's it, well done!" apparently my waters broke and he was born in seconds! I heard him cry, I saw his face. Seemed as if he was screaming his lungs out. It was then that I knew I had become a mother at last! I had my own precious baby that nobody can take away. To love and protect him forever.

He was wrapped up in a little blanket, unwashed, blonde hair and was the most perfect little baby. Naturally I counted every toe, every finger and kissed him on the forehead. He wrapped his little fingers around my finger, I could have held my baby in my arms forever. A nurse came in and informed me she was going to wash him, check his weight and all of him and another nurse would be taking me to be washed ready to go to my ward. Well I didn't want them to take him…ever, but working in the maternity ward at Shoalhaven hospital I understood why. She assured me that the baby would be brought back once I settled into the ward. After showering and settling into my bed in the four bed ward I introduced myself to the other women in the room. As promised my baby bundle was brought back to me. First thing I noticed was his hair, or rather lack of it.

"Where's my baby's blonde hair?" staring at the nurse, not impressed at all. She smiled as she carefully handed him to me.

"He had a bath, but he's still a beautiful baby boy. I think he will have your blue eyes." Apparently, all babies have similar color eyes until about 6 weeks. But this nurse was convinced he would have my eyes. Just as she was leaving my mum showed up. Mum cradled his head and kissed him, then blessed him with the Father, the Son and the Holy Ghost. She recited a few Christian words over his head and cuddled him.

"He's perfect, his nails are very long, that's a sign that he was overdue."

"Yes I told everyone bubs were overdue and no one believed me. But he is here now and I love him forever." I gently handed him over to her and she just held him for the entire time she was there. Shane turned up in the afternoon, he must have driven like a maniac. I was so pleased to see him. He had been by my side literally since I was 3 months pregnant, through the morning sickness, helping me get through Barrie's medical situation when I really needed someone on my side. Shane and I had already discussed our future; despite the fact that we were both very young we made our own choices together. Considering I had legally changed my surname to Walker, for this baby and for Barrie. Shane and I together made the decision to register the baby's surname as 'Layt'. We also intended to inform Barrie of this fact. When we were deciding on names, Bradley was my choice. During that year in May 1975, I had lost my cousin who was killed by a shark at Port Lincoln, South Australia. Brent was seventeen and it would have been his eighteenth birthday. He was also born on 24th November. Therefore, out of respect and great childhood memories, we added Brent to his name as a middle name. So the decision was made, this beautiful child was to be named and registered as: Bradley-Shane Brent Layt. Signed and sealed, done and dusted. Shane was so convinced that we would be married and I would be: Mrs. Marsha Layt.

Shane and I moved into a house together in Sydney, we actually shared the property with his mate Peter and his girlfriend Colleen. They had their own section to use but we shared the backyard mowing (ha-ha), BBQ and we did have some awesome parties with loud music. ABBA was the main band during the 70s and 80s The music was incredible and everyone knew the words. We sang to them, danced to them. Life was great. Shane and I used to win at dancing competitions, a great team. As a new mum, the day I came out of the hospital with my precious baby we could only stay a few hours with my family, in the afternoon I was suddenly in Shane's car, bubs in tow and we were on our way to Sydney to our new residence, a new town, no family. I had never even seen the house; in fact, I would have preferred to stay with my mum for at least a month. Both Shane and my mum were excited about the move. I definitely felt that I didn't get a say in the matter, it was a done deal. It was what it was. I hardly had time to settle into a routine with Bradley, with so many friends and family of Shane's popping in at all hours. I literally was exhausted by the end of his last night feed. It was only then that I appreciated the ten days in the hospital. I recall by day five being bored and starting to write a story about a vampire that sucked blood only from pregnant women. The nurses thought it was weird. Well, I was bored and just wanted to go home to mum.

As soon as I would close my eyes to snooze. Bradley would wake up crying. The bassinet was always on my side of the bed, so I could tend to him. The middle of the night was no fun for me. One time I swaddled him up nice and cozy in the bed with me to rock him to sleep. When Shane woke up at 4am for work I couldn't find my baby! I jumped out of bed screaming for Shane who was in the shower and couldn't hear me. Pulling the bed apart in a frenzy. Right at the bottom of the bed, there was my bundle of joy all snug and breathing fine. My heart was thumping so fast, I just grabbed him and went down to the kitchen to make a cup of tea. Shane had just come out of the bathroom and I told him what happened. Shane immediately took him out of my arms to check him over, cooing and cuddling him.

"Aww how's daddy's little man? All better now." He kissed him gently on his head, handed him back to me, and proceeded to get ready for work.

That day I made a pact with myself that I would get out of bed when Bradley woke up and go out to the lounge to feed him. Shane always made me a cup of tea. Of course, I was hanging for a 2SM, as we would say, but as I was breastfeeding it was off limits. On a visit to the post-natal checkups with the nurses they told me he had lost a bit of his birth weight, but quickly added that it was normal and not to worry about it. I thought to myself, then why bring it up. I was then stressing that I wasn't feeding him enough. She gave me forms with breastfeeding info, like how much each side, how long each side and how many wet nappies etc. Well that's like what I did at work, so I knew what they meant. Feeling a bit depressed and every two weeks I had to visit the nurse to get Bradley checked it only made me more depressed and hopeless. My breasts were slowly losing their milk. I was not sleeping and was tired all the time. Fay, my mother-in-law was very good to me and loved me bringing the baby around. Her husband absolutely adored Bradley- Shane.

He was sometimes a grumpy man; however, nothing was too much bother for the baby. They definitely had a special bond and it was good to see them together. By the time Bradley was six weeks old he was on part formula and each time I saw the CAFHS nurse the formula increased until he had been totally weaned off breast milk. There were some advantages, he drank more, gained weight, slept longer overnight and Shane and I were getting back to normal sleep. We even managed to get back to date nights as others could bottle feed him, like family members. One weekend we drove to my sister's place at Oak Flats. My niece had long blonde hair like me with a perm. Whilst I was rocking Bradley in the bassinet, my niece took over and he remained asleep. Yay! Kerri put her hand gently on his back. Shane and I slipped out the front door and quickly went to Albion Park to meet up with the couple we met at the hospital in Birilee. Christine had her daughter the night before I had Bradley.

Elizabeth was born at 7.20pm on 23rd November, Bradley was born at 7.15am on 24th November, almost twelve hours apart.

The four of us went horse riding somewhere out the back of Dapto. Of course, I was the 'princess' who had to be wearing high heels! I had to keep my thighs firmly against the girth of my horse as my shoes wouldn't stay in the stirrups After our rigorous ride through the hillside we stopped to rest. Shane had to help me dismount as I had extremely painful welts on my inner thighs, red and blistered. I could barely walk and Shane needed to take care of my skin. It took a few weeks to get the swelling down and heal. For quite a while I walked around like John Wayne. Eventually, we laughed about it and we never went horse riding again! One of our granddaughters was quite good with horses. We did have a few BBQs at the house where we put Bradley in his bassinet outside with us and Derek, who was elected as 'Godfather', used to put beer on his dummy. Bradley would sit up in the bassinet and literally squeal and dance with his arms to the music. His favourite song was ABBA's 'Fernando' trying to hum or sing it, and clap his hands when he heard it. He was a happy baby and everyone spoiled him. He grew up with our friends, family, and generally happy times. The main person in Bradley's life apart from Shane was Derek. To this day Bradley is still in contact with Derek, despite being in different states of Australia. When Bradley was about six months old I contacted Donna and Helmut who lived in South Nowra to arrange a meeting with Barrie at their place. I was informed he wasn't in the hospital. Shane and I wanted Barrie to see Bradley. This was arranged and very little information on his current health condition was given to either Shane or me. Usually, it would keep me up to date.

It wasn't until a few years later that some important and totally unexpected news came to light. I think, I know, that if I had known this information at the time, I fear my reaction would have been different. Shane and I made the long trip to the south coast with the baby in tow. Not sure how Shane personally felt at the time during the drive down, but it was definitely a bittersweet reaction for me. Apprehensive about having Barrie have his first time with his son, and deep down about his health status at the time. Of course, I was concerned with Shane's reaction to seeing Bradley finally in his bio dad's arms. I was hoping that I didn't start to cry if Barrie was unwell, like at death's door. Well the trip down seemed ok, no deadly silence as we chatted like usual. As we drove up the old road where the gate was to the entrance of Donna's farm, I could see Barrie, just standing there waiting. He looked well, perhaps lost a bit of weight, but generally looked no different since I had seen him when I was pregnant. Shane and Barrie had a reasonably civil conversation at meeting. Barrie put his arms out to for my bundle of joy, who was a little chubby at six months. Shane took a couple of Polaroid photos of them. I kept one of me holding Bradley – Shane.

Years later a friend borrowed the photo but never returned it. He passed away before I could get it back. I have no idea what happened to the other photo as Barrie had it and it would have been awesome to keep for Bradley as an adult. But there are no negatives on Polaroid photos. Barrie was pleased to meet Shane and knew he would take care of Bradley and me. I had no knowledge that Barrie had fathered a daughter, six weeks older than Bradley. I did the math.

That was the last time I saw Barrie. I only heard general information from my mum and dad until he passed away on 13th September 1978. He was only 34 years old. His wife sent me $100 for Bradley via my mum. Shane and I cruised along over the years, we had a couple of breakups ups and in the beginning really only minor events. We still loved each other and he still absolutely adored Bradley- Shane, in fact he would do anything for that little boy. I really don't know what the real issues were, we had a few legal issues to deal with at the time. I had to return to work, and as per usual, had to apply to the Nurses Board NSW, again, and was a bit nervous about what they would say this time. There was never a time when I never get a job in nursing, but each time I had to work back up to where I had left off. The hard yards all over again, personal care, showering difficult patients, sweating in the bathrooms and wards with no air conditioning. Early morning starts, limited breaks during the day. There was no such thing as lifters or even OHS legislation so we had to lift the patients ourselves. Later on in years as a trained and qualified nurse, I was the first to put my hand up for OHS representative. At every hospital from then on, I was elected and knew everything about every policy! Changed a few too, now they call it Manual Handling!

Even though it was physically draining being a nurse, especially a nurse assistant, you had to put your back and legs into it …. literally. By the time Manual Handling had been legislated, I was fully qualified and teaching others the right way so there were fewer injuries for nursing staff. Getting up very early in the mornings to get Bradley – Shane ready for childcare was draining and getting buses in the dark. At one point my sister in law would babysit for me. Either Shane or I would collect him, we actually worked well together as parents. In all honesty, I absolutely detested having to go back to work and leave my little boy all day. I would cry on the bus on the way to the hospital. I began to resent Shane for making me go back to work so soon, but we needed the money. That was just how it was back then. Feeling tired all the time however, I was appreciative of Shane caring for our little man, but he did little of anything else. I guess that too was the way it was in the 70s!

There were times when his mates would take over the time that he should have spent with me, as a family. However, Derek was becoming a third wheel in our relationship. His other mate would pop over now and then, filling a void. I believe this was the beginning of the end. I tried to ignore the signs. On one of our 'breakups,' I had taken Bradley back to Warilla near my family. One weekend, quite out of the blue, the RAAF guy, Glenn, turned up at my flat. He said he came to see how Bradley was and how I was coping. I actually was shocked to see him, but a good shock, I didn't even know he had my address. Perhaps Derek gave it to him, being the Godfather he would visit him often. Ironic as I felt Derek impacted my relationship with Shane too much, but he was great with Bradley, everyone loved him. The butterflies were back, no mistaking it or ignoring the feeling. I gestured Glenn inside and told him the baby was in his cot. Now it was only a one-bedroom flat, near the beach as usual, he asked if he could go in and pick him up, I nodded and was in the kitchenette putting the kettle on for our coffees. Just as I was doing this, there was a really loud bang on the door. As I went to see who it was, Shane just burst through the door and yelled,

"Where is he?" At the time I thought Shane was talking about the baby, before I could answer him, Glenn came out of the bedroom holding Bradley! OMG this wasn't going to look good. Shane was furious and told Glenn to get out and go home! I was pretty annoyed at his attitude and grabbed Bradley out of Glenn's arms. The yelling was scaring the baby and in fact, it was scaring me too. My head going blank, cramps with nerves in my abdomen.

I thanked Glenn for coming down and apologized for Shane's behavior.

As it was not Shane's place to say who could visit and who couldn't, he knew by my face that I was very angry with him. He never got that worked up when Derek, Bob or Bill popped in to see Bradley. I told Shane to leave, and he did. From that incident it changed us forever, whether we ever admitted it to ourselves or not. We eventually reunited more than once for a few months plus we had some privacy from his mates until we were back on track. We got engaged and both sides of our families were very pleased for us. Bradley – Shane was about 15 months old when we got married. All his mates were at the wedding party and they made all the plans. Shane and Glenn seemed to be ok and back on track. Apparently not quite. Ten days prior to the wedding the guys were meeting up at 7pm to have a night out. No drama about that. The girls in the apartment block where we lived in Cabramatta NSW, were going to have a bit of a party for me as we had all the kids and no babysitters! I was home during the day and just put Bradley down for his nap when there was a tap at the door. The RAAF guy was at the door with a smile on his face. He wanted to come in and said it was important. I asked him to be quiet as Bradley was asleep.

He came in and had a coffee with me. We put some music on and he chose Elvis Presley as he was very popular, this was 19th January 1977. He died in August 1977. Many of the songs we played burned into my heart for many years to come. A lot was said between us that doesn't need to be written here, but he was charming, persistent and it was quite clear that he wanted to be with me, as the song played in the background, 'It's Now or Never' .... long story short, it was NEVER. After a few hours, he eventually left and we never spoke of it again.... well for ages. He managed to turn up that night for the guy's night out, I was absolutely devastated by the impossible situation he had put me in just prior to my wedding to his best friend! He was the best man as selected as the Best Man, very awkward now indeed. He had made his declaration too late. Having said that, whenever I was in times of stress or needed a friend Glenn was always there to listen.

For a long time, his sister used to drive me crazy. I didn't like her and never trusted her around Shane. Everyone just laughed it off. I only tolerated her as she was Glenn's sister. Years later it was proven that I did have something to be concerned about. But it just made me feel like I had missed my chance. Life went on. The morning of my wedding I was with my parents just before walking down the aisle (which incidentally was my hallway) I broke down into tears. Dad put his arms around me and tried to comfort me. I told my dad the reason why. My mum was insistent that I was going to marry Shane and have a bloody happy life! So I proceeded down the hall into the lounge where the Marriage Celebrant was waiting. She looked at everyone gathered and asked,

"Is there anybody here who knows any reason why these two shouldn't be married, speak now ......"

I held my breath as I turned to the Best Man and the Groomsmen, they were all looking at each other. No one said a word. Complete silence except for some shoe shuffling. Phew. The Marriage Celebrant continued and when it came to the wedding rings, Glenn went to hand the rings over and accidentally put one on my finger. Quickly corrected himself, unnoticed by Shane, but the other guys saw it. Shane proudly put it on my wedding finger. The deal was done. I had promised him so much and I truly meant my vows. My mum was the first one to give Shane a congratulations kiss.

We had a quiet wedding and a simple reception. Nothing to rave about, I didn't ask for much and that's what I got.... That actually summed up my marriage with Shane. Maybe I should have asked for more, we had some good times and definitely some not-so-good times. Looking back, I don't know if we were too young or if I expected more from a marriage. I know I never wanted another marriage like my first one. Domestic Violence wasn't talked about a lot in those days, not like now in 2024! Now the DV mostly ends in murdering the spouse. I was inches away on several occasions from being another Statistic in the news. The memories are still vivid in my mind, such as being choked and passed out, fortunately, the feelings of dread, terror, and pain have managed to disappear from my head. Some things like actually being strangled and woken by two Paramedics doing CPR, shit that was scary! One time in 1979 I was upset over something, I cannot recall what it was over, but I do definitely recall a doctor. Being called out and requested by an ex. Without any warning or consent, I was injected and not long after fell asleep. Slept all night, knocked completely out! I was not impressed at all.

These days an after-hours doctor wouldn't be called for DV it would be the Police. Oh how times were so different back then for women. Each time my life and or my children's lives were threatened I had to start all over again. This was the worst part for me, upheaval of everything, possessions, financially, emotionally, loss of independence, and damage to one's perspective on life in general. Building distrust, fear, and uncertainty of the future. In one incident I was kidnapped for 7 days! When I get the courage to write about it I will. Darkness and very black moments. So many things it is a wonder I survived at all. For some reason I always thought cheating was the ultimate deal breaker in a relationship, believe me, it is definitely on the list, just not the top of the list anymore. It may hurt the same, harder to repair from as bones heal, surgeries heal and good dental work is available. But losing babies while in vitro is so hard. After losing the second unborn baby due to violence from the father, I took him to court in Victoria! Unfortunately, he did not get jailed for murder or even manslaughter of an infant at 26 weeks pregnant, only fined $250 and an AVO for 12 months. Not sure what the consequences would be today in 2024. So many organizations today acknowledge and help women who have had stillbirths, miscarriages, and recognition by burials, but I had nothing. As I have mentioned before, 2 girls, 1974 at 23 weeks pregnant and 1982 at 26 weeks. So sad and with the last one at Williamstown Hospital, Victoria the Technician and Gynaecologist had to turn the screen away from me so I couldn't see the horrific image on the ultrasound sonogram.

I was informed the baby was a girl, and was a mess from the injuries, and no way she could survive. Within minutes I had an IV cannula inserted, without consultation or consent, and was quickly wheeled into the operating theatre, where incidentally I worked in the same operating theatres. Everything went black, no time for cramps just out like a light. These days an unborn baby at 26 weeks would be classed as viable and could be registered with Births, Deaths, and Marriages and have a burial. So many lost babies are heavenly angels in their mothers' hearts. I know of friends from College who were sent to an unmarried mothers institution in Sydney who had their babies adopted out, it was so cruel. To go through all that labor and they just take the newborns away, and the parents of the girl sign the adoption documents. No one really talks about that stolen generation of these children! Those mothers never forget their babies. Fortunately, these days' children or young adults can try to search for their parents. Sometimes it is a happy ending and sometimes it is not. DNA has been a Godsend, whereas the truth can be found with scientific facts, genetic results, and other biological tests. The survival of violence in my earlier adult years was remarkable, including mental torture, physical abuse, financial abuse, and sexual abuse. I had survived it all. Or did I? Does any woman really survive?

My dad never hit me, he did lecture us kids with his philosophy and go on and on, at times I would think, 'Hell Dad, just whack me over the head as mum does.' But always in a tongue-in-cheek attitude. In all honesty, I am so glad he didn't hit me. My brother Terry and dad were my absolute protectors in my life No matter what they always had my back. When my dad passed away in 1998 it was heartbreaking. Both my sons were by my side along with my two brothers, Tom and Terry. I don't think I cried that much for so long, it really affected me and everyone in the family was sad too, especially all the grandchildren. He was an amazing and loving grandfather. The family was as society would call it these days a ' blended family'. Back in my growing-up days it was more of a 'don't tell the neighbors' or 'We are all family'.

The immediate family that I grew up with in the same household consisted of Mum, Dad, brothers Terry and Tom, and sisters Wendy and Margaret. Wendy lived with her mother in Victoria, and married young and we saw a lot of her. It was fantastic having her stay and I was lucky to get to stay with her and her husband Eddie while I was growing up. So many fun times and then with her little children as they came along. I do remember visiting her mother and I was a bit wary, her house seemed dark, dimly lit and she was in a wheelchair. Obviously I was too young to know about Polio and medical issues. It always stuck in my mind. At school we did get big needles to vaccinate us against Polio and later we got a spoon of pink Sabin to vaccinate against it. Phew! I wasn't a fan of that big stainless steel syringe! Wendy's husband was the most hilarious person you could meet. Eddie would play pranks on my mum and despite this, my mum loved him and they had a great relationship. Such a joker and pulled pranks on everyone.

So that was my family as I knew it. Two brothers, two sisters and I was the one in the middle. Not to forget the loving and protective German Shepherd dog, Tuppence. In retrospect, we seemed the perfect family. Education for me was always private Catholic Schools, both Primary and Secondary. Both run by nuns, which I have mentioned were cane happy. In today's world it would be classed as child abuse, nobody not even parents can hit a child of any age. Unfortunately, I don't really think the Government meant we couldn't discipline children, but that's not how they grew up. Times certainly became worse… children thieved, injured the elderly, murdered and there appeared no consequences and this was the end of manners, respect for conscience, acts of good, and no discipline by parents. Now those children are adults and their children have no knowledge of consequences either, so generations are participating in bad behavior. Free range and society are paying dearly for it. That is straight up my personal opinion re the kids of today of course the many hundreds of people I've met over the years have similar views.

Luckily our family had good parents, and we passed on those consequences. However, some were not as strict. The Government stuck its nose into family matters and declared that the extremists punished the majority, and the minority has taken over. No police control, nowhere to put them anyway. Parents are being punished for disciplining their own children and so it goes on. The world has gone mad, PC this and PC that, it's gone too far. There are still Pedophiles out there abusing children and they aren't all catholic priests either. No consequences? Lawyers get the family history to match up with the offender to get sympathy, father was a drunk, mother beaten in front of children, an unsavory uncle in the family, poor socioenvironmental lifestyle .....blah blah. This all leads up to poor mental health, generational behaviors and genetic. I personally was subject to a spanking or two, welts on my legs from willow switches and belts. Fortunately, I attended a private Girls' College and we were covered head to toe with our uniforms so no one knew.

The welts, cuts, and bruises were unseen! Were we the lucky ones? As years went by unfortunately the circle of life or generational behavior carried on. So I guess it saved my grandchildren, what about the ones it didn't save or the 'bad seeds'? Why the increase in theft, murders, and sexual abuse? We all know it's wrong and you could go to jail, why the increase? No consequences for the young generation these days! Who is looking out for the good guys? The elderly? The vulnerable? Whilst I was studying at Wollongong University as an undergraduate Registered Nurse, and still working as an Enrolled Nurse there, there were spates of elderly people being found dead in their own homes in Sydney, a populated area. TV reporters were telling us that some had been dead for months and no one noticed. Despite the accumulating newspapers on lawns or driveways, letterboxes spilling over with letters. Some had electricity disconnected through nonpayment including telephones and Gas accounts. Dead people can't pay bills. This was heartbreaking and no one seemed concerned in this populated thriving city. So what went wrong?

Researching into the deaths, lifestyles of the elderly, and seeking a better outcome. Who had a duty of care? Who should have noticed these people were no longer interacting within the community? I actually took weeks looking into this sad event happening amongst the crowd. Why not notice? Are people in society too afraid to be involved with their neighbors? These unfortunate elderly people were not murdered or robbed in a home invasion. They simply died because no one noticed them, as if they were invisible. No family or friends. This fed my curiosity and sense of compassion. I contacted the Federal Health Minister by email and was very disappointed by the attitude!

"Not our problem, it is a State issue...." basically was the answer. The state Health Minister was not much help either. It seemed no one cared or was taking any responsibility. I wasn't stopping there! I prepared my research into a full-on documentation, put it on a floppy disc, and later on a CD. It took me a while, in between studying, working hard as an EN to complete the undergraduate degree but my determination helped me edit the data ready for the Government of the day to put forth my recommendations.

It felt strange being in the Federal Member of Parliament, Jenny George MP, with my policy proposal. Approaching the receptionist's desk who barely looked up at me,

"Can I assist you?" I informed her that I had something for her, to which she replied,

"I am sorry Ms. George is quite busy, can I offer you an appointment in two weeks when she is back from Canberra.?

"No thank you, I need to see her before her trip to Canberra. It is ok I can sit and wait all day." I proceeded to make myself comfortable in one of the chairs in the waiting area. The receptionist appeared a tad annoyed with me, however within ten minutes or so I was in Jenni George's office. We chatted a few minutes and I thought it would be more nerve-racking, in fact it went well. She briefly looked over my cover letter, read the main issues, and my proposals. Ms. George MP looked up at me paused for a moment then asked, "Were you ever in Adelaide at a Nurses Conference, as a Conference Delegate?"

I nodded, feeling a bit embarrassed.

"Yes I was actually." Recalling vividly the Conference she mentioned. I was representing SA nurses in the Aged Care sector on that particular occasion as an Enrolled General Nurse. I had previously been involved in a 'Workload Survey' in NSW at Sutherland Hospital. It was called The Reasonable Workloads Survey and was completed on my ward and very successful whereas the Director of Nursing requested me to survey the entire Hospital, including the Emergency Department. The survey was a huge undertaking and I was very passionate about it. Taking a lot of discipline and professionalism, the outcome assisted directly into reshaping workloads and ratios for nurses and patients.

At this particular conference my role was to speak about ratios and workloads with the then Federal Health Minister. He began his speech, then polishing off a glass of red from a bottle our table had one won, I let him be aware that totally disagreed with him and mention the Reasonable Workloads Survey across an entire general hospital. Every one of the nurses cheered. Not sure if my passion helped or the glass of red !I knew exactly what Ms. George MP referred.

She smiled at me and continued, "You are a bit of a mover and shaker …"

Ms. Jenny George MP agreed to take my disc and documents to Canberra. I was absolutely thrilled. This meant more to me than anyone realized. Someone in Parliament was going to listen to me in regards to the elderly dying unnecessary in their own communities. I felt I had given it my best shot to bring about change for a better outcome.

The general outcomes were pleasing as there were more alerts on data bases and community follow ups. There were some resistance by small groups who pointed out some elderly didn't like neighbors knowing their business. However, I did prove that GP's, Pharmacists, Community organizations and Allied Health had a duty of care to the vulnerable. The changes worked, for example:

If an elderly person (or couple) suddenly stop getting a script refilled like cardiac medication, if the pharmacy has not refilled the script or seen them within that time frame then the GP gets an alert, the Pharmacist gets an alert etc. it's not being nosey, just a duty of care for their health and welfare. Mind you when I became an RN and worked at clinical and management level I realized how much data collecting there is to be done. Very daunting when doing projects analyzing all that data for government departments who most likely won't do anything with it. Oh well I got paid well for my effort.

Chapter 5:
Continual Nursing Skills.

As a District Nurse in regional Victoria it was bittersweet. The patients were awesome and always welcoming, the actual staff were not always the friendliest. Especially the one that was, well she thought she was in charge. In fact, she was second in charge. Unfortunately, the top boss did whatever the 2IC wanted. Fortunately, I worked well with the managers in other departments. Palliative Care nursing within the community was extremely rewarding and I worked my way up to being the most skilled in that area. The nurse in charge was a wonderful mentor to me, not only recognizing my update skills but my passion for oncology, palliative care and end of life nursing. This enable be to attend and participate in many conferences, workshops and being the on call Palliative Care nurse for after hours for the entire district. My purposeful hospital vehicle was supplied with many medical supplies and access to medications for my patients. This included morphine, chemotherapy and cytotoxic equipment and PPE (Personal Protection Equipment).

Due to my training and experience in mental health I also managed the clients with specific medications that required strict monitoring and supply of same. This I enjoyed also, I tried to educate the team the importance of some medications for mental health clients were carefully monitored and therefore less risk of relapse. Disappointingly they weren't that keen on 'mental health' issues displaying no regard for duty of care. Obviously it became easier to put me in charge of all mental health clients, the community Mental Health Team and liaison with the pharmacists than the other nurses deal with it. I regarded those team members as discriminating and setting a bad example for the new nurses. The stigma was outrageous. Then there was the issue of OH&S, there was none in our section. So once again I was elected as OH&S representative, which turned out well as it gave me powers to enforce policies and a new forum with other representatives from all hospital wards. Having complete autonomy and legislations to back me up. The people I met were fantastic, very professional and we still keep in touch today, 14 years later!

The conferences were usually in Melbourne or in Bairnsdale so Motels were tax deductible. I always got paid for going to a conference, absolutely fantastic. It was during my trip to Bairnsdale that I went to the cemetery seeking to locate my maternal great grandparents. Caroline and Martin Carpenter died very young, 34 years and 35 years respectfully in 1906. Sadly, there were only markers of the really older graves. No headstones or graves as such. The Markers were like rusty old metal sticks in the ground with no names. The ones that did have names on blocks of cement or grave stones were sad. Babies died early, most children didn't live past 5 years of age. Adults died under the age of 58 yrs. The weather that particular day was over 40 degrees and walked around the entire cemetery searching for my great grandparents. It wasn't just sweat rolling down my face, it was tears, heavy sobs, searching with overwhelming sadness. Sitting on a mound of dirt and prayed to my nana Crosbie, at least I had tried to locate her mother and father with a heavy heart failed.

This leads me back to my earlier note regards to cremation Vs burial. If my great grandparents and grandparents were cremated would I have their ashes? Would someone else in the family, distant relative have them? I don't know but I would think my sister Kathy and I would have liked to have Caroline Carpenter and nana's ashes. We would share time with them with respect. So ultimately there was a no show at the Bairnsdale Cemetery. I do recall the sadness walking through and reading the names and ages of the young children. I never went back. Oddly enough when I was telling one of the nurses at work the 'boss' the 2IC pops over,

"Oh you are from around here?" she looked so surprised when I explained about my family history. Almost immediately her faced softened and she seemed a lot more interested in me, not classed as an outsider but now a local. Amazingly my treatment became a lot better, more inclusive, improved duty roster. my mindset was still 'keep your friends close and your enemies closer' That is just the way I am and always will be.

When I first started my nursing career 16 yrs. and 8 months, the nursing profession was completely different. Harder to get into and student nurses were proud of their achievements, more compassionate, and listened to those who were skilled and literally in charge of them. There were skills you had to master or you would repeat, repeat and repeat until you got it correct. These Masteries had to be signed off as complete, not just turn up and have a crack! It was very serious task participation in front of not just your peers but in front of senior Registered Nurses and or Matron. We all know nothing gets past the Matrons! Such basic skills on making a strictly wrinkle free bed. Envelope corners on beds, including the center tuck at end of the bed as not to cause pressure sores on feet. Patients tended to stay in their beds back in the day, waiting for doctor's rounds or nursing staff to attend to vital observations. Everything was documented before rounds and reported to the nurse in charge. Abnormal readings were reported by the RN to the Matron. The doctors team were notified and any instructions or changes were documented and orders followed. It seemed a good system. The Matron knew every staff member, every patient including their medical status and all the doctors on staff. Matron was always in charge.

During my first week of nursing I encountered a scary sight. Victor Harbor South Coast Hospital had an annex at the time where elderly patients were admitted while waiting a bed in a specific ward or awaiting discharge. This particular evening an elderly gentleman, who was being restless, aggressive and uncooperative was tied (restrained) to his hospital bed for his safety and safety of others. From memory he had a security guard or an orderly, like a wards man and then HASA as the years went on. The initial shock of the sight of this man still attached to this wrought iron bed, walking upright with the bed on the back of him yelling and walking towards the door! There were about three of us student nurses and we ran to the nurse's office screaming for help. Many nurses, security and wards men came rushing in restrained him, or rather the bed and a senior nurse gave him an injection. Within a few minutes he was subdued and his bed was put back in place, at that point that had been the scariest thing I had ever seen. Matron was extremely supportive of us girls witnessing this behavior and had a debriefing with her.

Working in the General hospitals over the first five years of nursing wasn't too bad. I always felt supported, well educated in which ever ward I happen to be on. In those days from 1972 till maybe late 90's there were women's medical ward, women's surgical ward, men's medical and men's surgical etc. Separate wards which I preferred that way, as a nurse and as a patient. These days' wards are mixed and surgical, medical, neuro etc. however Maternity only had women but unfortunately women who have had miscarriages or lost a near term stillborn were admitted to this ward. You could hear the newborns cry which was upsetting for them to hear. One clinical maternity practicum as a trainee Enrolled nurse in a regional area in NSW I experienced a really sad birth indeed. This pregnant young lady came in with severe contractions but was only 28 weeks' gestation. The fetus had died four weeks ago and the Gynecologist insisted she carry it till full term. Unfortunately started early and mother nature made the decision. The entire Greek family were there yelling at her as if it was her fault and evil.

An emergency caesarean eventually emerged a dreadful outcome, even I was horrified! The deceased fetus was black, shaped like a baby but congealed. Apparently the Medical photographer took photos for medical journals and teaching purposes. It was absolutely horrific to look at and I felt so sorry for the young Greek lady for her loss. She was now getting verbally abused by her Greek family members on her husband's side. The remains of this charred little body was taken to a lab in Sydney most likely Glebe Coroners. The doctors were discussing the situation with interns and nursing staff. I only recall one time where the doctors and nurses briefly spoke with the traumatized mum. The vast numbers of the Greek community and family were now gathered in a waiting room away from the mother. The husband told his family that his wife is no longer welcome in his home. He also told them that she was the devil to produce such a child! After that night she was abandoned, disowned, and homeless, all the staff were hoping for a social worker and an interpreter to help her. Where was the justice for this woman?

After this tragic event it took many months to sleep at night, visions of that charred body. But nurses in general are taught how to cope, to be 'professional' but we can't always be hard-hearted, and unaffected by the tragic and horrific sights we see. It can't be unseen. Another nursing incident I witnessed was almost as bad. This was in a city nursing home and oddly enough there were over 50 % Asian descent residents, normally the Asians were very good at looking after their elderly parents. I was working casually for an agency Monday to Friday getting up early in the morning when it was still dark driving to work. I had to leave my six children to safely get to school on their own. I had a horrible job in a horrible nursing home, which had been shut down several times and reopened in a different name. I was always wet with sweat showering up to ten residents in a short timeframe. Again my boots were saturated and there were no windows in the bathrooms that opened. Often I had to catch my glasses from falling off. I was tired, had no breaks it was a nightmare! You just went from one person to another and after you had finished then you had to make the bed with NO clean sheets and of course no clean towels.

I actually broke down one day and told my husband what I had seen that shift. An elderly frail lady is continually calling out from her bed. I was told to get her up and shower her. I pulled back the bed linen only to reveal her leg. From her foot to her upper thigh was glistening dark green almost black! OMG, it was full-on gangrene. I was almost sick. This poor woman must have been in agony! I covered her up and ran out to find an RN to help, even pain medication before a shower and something to wrap up her leg. No one helped. There were no medications written up for her. I couldn't believe it, just couldn't. I actually tried to call a doctor for some pain relief PRN, but no help. So all I could do at that moment was to wrap her leg in a bin liner secured by micro pore tape as gently as I could. She screamed the entire time in the shower. I prayed that God would take her that night. After speaking to my husband about it, I never went back. This occurred in early 1990 and still haunts me to this day.

In reflection there were some good nursing memories that did make my carerworthwhile. I enjoyed surgical nursing where I could see literally skin regrow and heal. Cells become full tissues of skin. Patients healing from surgery or trauma and being discharged home. It was such a good outcome and I am proud of your work. Rehabilitation was another area that I enjoyed working full-time. The staff were fantastic, all on the same page as it were. The goal being to help the patients to be independent and well enough to go home. Some were physical and some were there due to accidental trauma injuries, spinal injuries, car accidents, falls from roofs etc. Some had permanent injuries but after rehabilitation, were able to live the best possible lives with their disability. In a spinal unit in Adelaide, I nursed a young woman in her early 20s, both her legs were like tree trunks and I say that in a caring way. She was permanently on her back unable to move her heavy legs, it took four nurses to care for her, move her into a bath bed. Unfortunately she had no feelings in her legs and very awkward using the lifting machine. At that point there weren't many if any that I recall back then were Bariatric beds, everything was hard yards, no wheelchairs wide enough or even strong enough for large weights. Back in the 80's it was hard yakka to say the least. We were all taught in nursing school,

"Use your legs, hold it your guts and lift with your legs." Naturally Manual Handling has replaced old school of thought, and decreased Work Cover injuries. Many nurses went off the profession or retrained in another area such as a desk job. The nursing teams, doctor's teams and specialists would get together monthly to discuss the situation around the patients bed and included the patient.

It was at one of these collaborative team meetings was with the bed bound lady who had been for most of her life and was in regards to her quality of life. Her best options were the discussion of the month. Many Orthopedic surgeons and other professional

84

medical personal were invited. Family members also acted on behalf of the patient, let's call her Tracey. Many ideas were put forth until at the next meeting an outcome was presented and a decision had to be made by the patient. The first time I hears the option presented, I was absolutely shocked, horrified actually. Thinking that it was outrageous and cruel. Many specialists, surgical staff high in their field and even a couple of overseas specialists were involved. The plan was to amputate both legs above the knee. This giving her the opportunity to be ambulant in a wheelchair especially designed for her without the weight of her legs. I think the words used were, "Nonfunctioning limbs".

After post op rehabilitation and ready for a new life, Tracy got a small downstairs Housing Department unit and her wheelchair fitted perfectly, she was independent and loving life. Now having the ability to go out and meet people she discovered so many new friends. I realized that it was the best option for her after all. No longer living or should I say existing in a huge Spinal Unit with 24 hour care, she was free! I saw her one day in the city in her new wheelchair, she waved and I went up and gave her a big hug. She was rocking a new hairstyle too, short with pink and purple highlights. She looked amazing and was so happy. Tracy had been handing out newsletters for the Community Disability Sector, and she loved her new forever independence. It made me realize you don't need to be 100% able bodied to be 100% independent. Having assistance to do things doesn't take away your independence, it actually enhances your independence, plus it allows you to have a lifestyle to live a lifestyle! I have encouraged many of my patients over the years during their rehabilitation to look outside the square and see where you fit. Later on in years I undertook a course to specialize as a Rehabilitation Nurse.

To all those newbie nursing students out there studying nursing either as an Enrolled General Nurse or a Registered General Nurse, there are so many enjoyable and fulfilling nursing jobs out there to do. Make the most of your Clinical Practical's, try something outside the square ! Be part of the change in healthcare. I have a dear friend who we worked together in a nursing home for many years. I got out and worked in Management roles in a different area of nursing. Eventually my friend left too and obtained a job, she now teaches nursing at TAFE and is so happy in her job role. Absolutely loving her job and changed her lifestyle 100%. So have a go, there are so many areas in health to be part of the change!

Growing up in the 60's and 70's was generally good and life for me was cruisy, the beach walks, the sand, fishing in the lake at Winding, lake Illawarra, with my dad. Watching brilliant sunsets and hanging out with my friends. As I am feeling emotionally stronger and more stable I can now decanter some of the dark times in my earlier life. Events not so good, but should really come into its own chapter or as my dear friend Diana and I refer to as:

'You Can't Make This Shit Up.'

A deep breath. When I first found out my biological father was Theo George Nowak I went to meet him, as they say, curiosity killed the cat …His much younger wife and their son lived in Frankston Victoria, where I was actually born. I had an irreversible incident with my mum, one of many. Basically on my 14th birthday I had my first boy and girl mixed party, which was a big thing in those days. During the party the phone rang and I answered it, as it was my birthday after all! A man on the other end wished me a 'Happy 14th birthday' I thanked him and asked who he was, his reply changed my childhood forever!

"I am your father". I was speechless for a moment then explained my father was in the dining room. When the words hit me I went blank, couldn't hear, couldn't see, it was dark again. Had cramps in my tummy really bad and was hard to focus on anything. The music stopped playing, I recall asking my mum what it meant. My 'dad' as I knew him gave me a big hug and the next thing I knew I was being carted, escorted by force, to the neighbors across the road. All my friends had to leave the party and to this day I have no recollection on what was said or done during the next two days. It was totally blanked out in my head. Finally, my parents came over to take me home and it was a very strange conversation. A previous marriage, unhappy, bad man, etc., etc.,. My head was spinning, my thoughts were all over the place and nothing felt real. For a few months I was getting nasty letters from so called school friends in my letterbox.

"Marsha P. hasn't got a father."

"Marsha has no name."

As if to add insult to injury without even realizing I am 'damaged goods'. My mum took me aside one day and quietly told me about this 'orphaned boy' about 16 years' old who lost both parents in a car crash.

Mum continued on to say that they were going to let him stay with us. Ok I thought as mum was always looking after someone's kids. My cousins stayed for ages when my aunt Mavis was unwell. So nothing unusual. A month later mum and I travelled to Melbourne which seemed in the middle of the night. We were in this huge gated building with security guards as I thought, as I was told it was an orphanage, not that I had ever seen one before, only on TV. It definitely was dark, cold, and scary. My heavy coat not taking the full Melbourne's winter weather. There stood a boy, a little taller than me with a smile on his face as he approached me across the concrete yard. As we got closer, my mum had a beautiful smile on her face, clearly pleased to see him. He approached me with his arms outstretched to hug me. I was a little, no actually, a lot taken aback by his openness. Then another irreversible moment, No. 2 hit me. Mum had tears cascading down her cheeks as she introduced me to my brother! There was a lot of hugging from both of them but I had my face hidden in his chest, so no one could see my reaction. Shock, tears, anger and sadness all at once. Things in my head went blank for a good few minutes. I could not process it at all.

We eventually had him back at our house in Warilla a few months later. Obviously there were some paperwork to complete, I never saw any of it. In the meantime I met Mr. Theo N. It was strange meeting him, everything was new and strange, like my first flight to anywhere. really loved flying. I have mentioned that I wanted to be an air hostess. Meeting Theo for the first time, well obviously not since I was 2 years old, was weird as them wasn't an instant connection. The same as when I met Kevin. His wife I could tell in an instant did not like me at all. Perhaps jealous, perhaps I looked too much like my mum, in any casewe weren't good together. Theo took me out a few times, just us two and it was nice, meeting his friends who obviously remembered me from a baby or a toddler. We even went to visit my brother in the orphanage, which in reality my bio dad explained it was a Government based Boys Home for ward of the state boys. The more I learnt the darker my mind became.

I learnt so many stories from my brother and Theo and I can tell you over 90% of these claims were verified by legal documents, court documents with I had read with my own eyes! So I didn't need to listen to the truth from others, as I had read it myself. A few days later another 'event' occurred, another life altering declaration. This one really hurt me the most. Theo and I were having lunch at his house when he casually asked how did I get along with my sister, Kathy. I looked at him amused and replied.

"You mean Margaret / Maggie don't you? She a great little sister, dark hair about 6 years old".

He looked straight at me with those dark deep eyes, sipped his coffee, and moved towards me from the sink.

"No I mean Kathy, Kathleen, your older sister." He raised an eyebrow and waited.

"No you're mistaken, Kathy is my aunt, like Aunt Mavis, except Kathy has red hair.

My mind seemed to go blank, black, foggy. Theo informed me without any malice in his voice or tone.

"Kathy is your sister, ask your mother for the truth. I may be a lot of things, but I am not a liar. She is truly your sister. Those words rang in my head. I couldn't breathe, I couldn't see, and something went wrong with my vision for a few moments. Unable to comprehend any of it anymore. It was just too much to bear at 14 years old. The cramps had returned. On the trip back to NSW I was in another world, my brain overloaded, overwhelmed and my heart broken. Thinking back to those wonderful days in Wangaratta, visiting my nana and pop and the little red-haired girl, who always wanted to play 'sisters'. I would always say,

"Oh yes that would be fun!" It was at that moment, in that plane 30.000 feet in the air, I realized that we were in fact sisters by the same mother! Three lies, who else knew? My mother, Theo, maybe Kevin, and for sure my nana and pop, aunt Mavis, and dad (stepdad) Oh goodness too many people.

I felt like a discarded piece of a puzzle. Wondering how Kathy must have felt growing up without or Kevin. I didn't know about him till I was 14 years of age. Not only not know, but mum had straight out lied to me. Absolutely! Mum told me my brother was an orphan, his parents killed in a car crash. OMG I have no name, and plenty of siblings. Was there more? My dad, the only dad I knew, picked me up from what I refer to from then on, my home station Oak Flats Station, Illawarra, Wollongong. There were many times in my growing-up years and even in my adult years that Dad was there to collect me and take me home. Anytime I wanted to come home, he always looked happy to see me. Every time. When he hugged me, I always felt better. As far as I know Dad had never lied to me. Dad and step-brother Terry, weird as I never ever referred to him as that, just my big brother, were the two main men in my life relying on then for truth, protection, love and support, no matter what the situation. When dad and I arrived home this day I requested he wait in the car for at least ten minutes. I only needed ten minutes.

Walking up the steps to the front door of my home I could hear a record playing. 'The Green Green Grass of Home' by Tom Jones 1967. My mum was smiling and had her arms outstretched to hug me. Everything went blank like a short circuit. I pushed mum against the wall just in an unstoppable rage, looking straight at her I yelled,

"Don't tell me any more lies! Who is Kathy? Who is she to me?" her face went pale, I moved away as tears were flowing… from me. Mum tried to say that 'Herbie' was telling lies to me, then mum had tears cascading down her beautiful face, her dark fox eyes filled with shame or regret. At last the truth is coming out, yes she was my sister, half-sister, different father. Naturally I have never to this day referred to Kathy as 'half-sister'. Apparently mum never married Kathy's father, she married Theo who 'promised' to adopt her. He didn't so he always got the blame. Theo was the biological father to both Kevin and myself, reflecting back to the DNA of siblings of same parentage. Feeling so overwhelmed and distraught with all this, and not 100% believing she was blameless. I took my shattered heart to my room for hours

Dad knocked on my door and I allowed him in. He sat for a long time and just listened to me of course he tried to make excuses for her actions and yet he understood how I felt betrayed. He hugged me, wiped my eyes and said in a comforting manner,

"In time when you are older and wiser you too will make mistakes or have regrets. But you must remember those that truly love you will always support you." He kissed my cheek and straightened my tangled blonde strands off my face.

"Thank you, I love you dad. I am only staying here for you." We hugged and he left the room. I fell into a deep sleep. Things were a bit estranged for a while but we tried to live a life the best way we could. At some point I went to stay with Theo for a very short time. His wife had set me up with some bullshit story to the Swan Hill Police. Had I mentioned Theo and his family had sold up in Frankston and moved to Swan Hill. So there was crap said about me, which was nonsense and still hold a grudge against her for that! Theo believed it, put me and my Glory Box on the next train to Oak Flats, of course where else! Dad was faithfully there to meet me. Home sweet home.

I am not sure of the timing, but I was still at St. Mary's College and Kevin was released from the 'Boys Home' and came to live with us at Warilla. My school friends all thought he was 'cute'. Ha-ha, if you are a young teen girl attending an all-girls school run by nuns, any 16 year old male would look 'cute'. Kevin and I were vastly different. I was forbidden to tell anyone he was my brother, forbidden to wear the locket that Theo and Kevin had bought me because it had my initials on it (MCN). God forbid if people found out my real name! The shame on the family, I would be sent straight to hell. Kevin got a job in Wyaralong and we went to the pictures, but we had a stop put on that behavior as I wasn't allowed to be alone with him. Seriously!! We got in trouble to listening to music in the front room, on the record player, LP's and EP's whatever they were it was frowned upon. The Beatles music considered to incite youngsters to go crazy. That so annoyed me. Elvis was a great hit back then, but not for me as mum said there was too much 'jiggling of the hips'. How ridiculous was that!

Kevin used to tell me his stories about his life in the younger days. He had so many memories about me that I knew nothing about. His abandonment issues, loss of his mother and her love growing up into adulthood in a boy's home. It still haunts me today of some information he spoke about. The older I became the easier it was to find the loopholes and enable me to find the truth. Before he came to live with us I used to be beaten with willow switches and I was quietly threatened of it happening again if I even uttered my birth name. So I didn't, and this upset Kevin a great deal. He really was furious and suspicious when my locket went missing. Just disappeared from the face of the earth! He believed mum had disposed of it so I wouldn't wear it and expose to everyone my real name. I think he was right. We never found it and we never mentioned it, only to each other. It stressed me out that I was 'Pope' to the outside world but 'Nowak' on anything legal, until I went for my learners permit at 17, I didn't realize I had to get my birth certificate. We both hated living this lie. It messed with my head, my identity, I felt I was nobody's child. I sensed Kevin was getting agitated and knew in my heart he would leave.

I begged him to take me with him. He explained that it was not the life for me. I was told that I was not 'streets smart' and too educated with a Christian upbringing and could not out run the Police! We both laughed at that. I guess he was right. Not long after that day we had that conversation, he was gone. The front door left open. I knew why. Immediately my mum called the Police to get him arrested. I was furious and didn't understand why get him arrested? I was so full of anger, he was MY brother and I admit I threw a hissy fit. I felt abandoned and not in control of this situation and why should I be? I don't know what happened, but I knew I had to leave to find my own niche in life. I contacted my nana in SA and asked if I could visit for a while. She said her and Grandpa Reynolds would love to have me stay. My beautiful nana Crosbie had passed away in the February, and this was about July. So I made plans to leave. Mum did not want me to go, but dad said,

"If you stop her from going, she'll never come back. So let her get it out of her system,"

So I went to Adelaide.

Chapter 6:
The start of recovery.

Living on the South Coast in Goolwa, SA was such a magical time for me. For six amazing weeks having fun in the sun, riding over sand dunes in a buggy with my grandparents and a young couple they knew. Life was fantastic, carefree and I loved the beach and the surf. As my nana knew the Matron at the local hospital she made enquiries regarding me doing my nursing training. Well that kicked off my nursing career, the 8th of August 1972 at 06:30 hrs. The hospital had just built a brand new Nurses' Quarters. All modern 20 rooms for 20 new student nurses. I had my own room, with a single bed, a built in wardrobe and desk with a mirror, a small bedside chest of drawers and a chair. The bedside chest and chair were the only items you could move around. All the rooms were the same style. There was a shower and toilet block including a bath. The laundry had an automatic washing machine, a dryer, sinks, and a cupboard with an ironing board and an iron. We had to launder our own uniforms. The laundry had an exit door which was nearby Matron's apartment, despite the closeness we would leave the laundry door unlocked if someone was coming home after curfew, being 10pm. Matron always knew what shift the nurses were on, she did the rosters and nothing slipped past her! So we had to be quiet as a mouse.

The kitchen and pantry was always well stacked with staples and foods. Although you didn't need to cook as the hospital had a main dining room for all Staff. The formal dining room was situated in between the hospital building and the nurses quarters and was open every day. There were some strict protocols for staff. If you were seated, having your meal and the Matron came in, you had to stand up and not able to sit until Matron had collected her meal and sat down at her table! That was a fact, this happened at every hospital I worked in during the 70's and 80's. It was a sign of respect. Top grade chefs prepared and cooked the meals, breakfast, lunch and dinner. There was a Bain Marie type server and each person would collect a tray and lined up with your plate, bowl, or whatever crockery and cutlery you required and present it and the server staff would serve whatever you wanted. I usually had 2 poached eggs on white toast, fried tomato and crunchy bacon. Sometimes I would have corn flakes for breakfast too! It came included in your board taken $10 per fortnight out of your pay if you lived in the Nurses Quarters. That was a pretty sweet deal. Those days have gone! Back in 1972 I would get as a nurse assistant / trainee $34.00 per fortnight after tax and board deducted. So I was pretty happy to have a new place to live, secure and close to work, eat well and a great bunch of nurses for company.

My room was usually a gathering spot on race days as you could see the finishing post from my window. We would put ten cents in the 'kitty' and if your chosen horse won, you got the 'kitty'. It was so much fun. I feel sorry for the modern-day student nurses, as we all helped each other learn, we were safe and cared for, the Matron and the housekeeper would keep an eye on us, it truly was the best life. One night there were a few of us home and we didn't know how to turn the gas heater on. I may have been involved in the suggestion of lighting the newspapers in the steel bin ... just maybe... Well we all thought it was a steel bin. We lit the fire, it melted the bin and scorched the new carpet underneath. Luckily they were carpet squares and we managed to move them around so they went under furniture to hide them .... Well that was the plan. Matron found out from the housekeeper within two days. All of us who were not on the roster working that night of the 'crime' were requested to front up Matrons office. We were scared our parents or worse the Police would be called. One by one we lined up outside Matrons office. One by one called into the office and interrogated. Nobody knew anything. That pay week we all had $1.12 deducted from our pays to cover the cost to replace the three carpet squares and a new bin. Matron informed us the bin was NOT fireproof. So there, this is a perfect example of the power of the Matron in that era! She could put you on a month's night duty if she wanted, deny a weekend off just to punish us. These days' newbies would be crying 'workplace bullying'. So this is how it was, we all accepted it and learnt the hard way. We also learnt greater skills and worked towards earning autonomy, not to mention we learnt how to turn a gas heater on. Ha-ha.

One surgical patient, a young man of 24 yrs., let's call him 'John', I recall he was a high school teacher at Port Elliot, he was good looking and charming. Long story short, a couple of student nurse smuggled in a bottle of vodka for him. Matron found out. The patient was 'dishonorably discharged', yes she could do that too. The two student nurses were given a right royal talking to, plus their parents were informed. It wasn't me, thank goodness. A week after his discharge he called the nurses' quarters phone and invited all the nurses to a party. Eighteen of us went. Two nurses were on duty that night. Some took lifts in cars, some he picked up himself, one way or another we all managed to get there. Yes, it was an awesome party and I was the last one to leave at 4.30 am, am not so sure if that's something to brag about. I snuck in the laundry door, quietly. I was immediately jumped on by four nurses and taken into the shower. Eventually we laughed about it.

After getting out of my saturated clothes, showered and into Pajamas could finally fall asleep by 5.20 am. I was rudely awakening by a loud knock on my door and then heard the key unlocked the door. I jumped up to see Matron standing there! She used her master key (kept for our safety) She was at the end of my bed with her arms folded. I feigned a toothache and apologized for the sleep in. According to Matron I had exactly ten minutes to get dressed and present myself to her office! Holy Hell. On presentation outside her office she made me wait a further ten minutes. No waiting chairs around as young ladies were to stand erect with hands behind their backs. Matron believed the toothache, which I did have a molar that needed attention two years ago. She gave me two paracetamol tablets, ordered me to rest until 1.30pm as she had kindly made an appointment with Mr. Blackburn the local dentist at 2pm. Did I mention Matrons' powers of autonomy? At 2pm she had driven me to Mr. Blackburn's dental surgery. My back molar was painfully extracted. On the drive home to the nurses quarters in her Holden Kingwood, she turned to me and said in a rather kind, motherly tone, but firm,

"Next time you go out partying, ensure you are home before 10pm, to have enough sleep for duty the next day." She knew the whole time!

I was both shocked and embarrassed, however had a smile on my face despite the numbness from the extraction. I stepped out of her car and quietly thanked her. Ok lesson learnt. After all, that I slept from 4pm to 5am, showered, dressed into full uniform, pinned on my fob watch and pinned my hair up. Now I ready for a hearty hot breakfast and go on duty by 6.30am Another day another dollar as my dad would say. Some weekends if I was rostered off duty I would take the opportunity to visit my grandparents in Goolwa. It was a great feeling hanging out with them as they were so good to me. My aunt Rosemary and my cousins would visit too and we had such a wonderful family get together, eating, laughing, swimming at the beach always being a happy childhood memory. It was nearing my 17th birthday and I brought home to Nana's one of the nurses who had become a really good friend. Jenny was a little older than I, almost twenty, and had begun her PTS nursing training. On meeting Jenny for the first time, the first thing nana said was,

"Oh dear, you need to lose a few pounds in weight". I was so embarrassed as I was only a size 6 and the biggest part of me were my boobs. But poor Jenny was at least three times the size of me with only half the boobs. I still think fondly of nana even years after she passed. Hey it was what it was. I loved nana but she did say some outrageous comments that either made me laugh or caused embarrassment. I probably said some funny ones too. I told my grandparents one visit that I had saved a person's life. They were very proud of me and asked what did I do? I unashamedly replied,

"I took their blood pressure!". They laughed for hours.

My birthday came and went. A few of us girls celebrated at the Crown Hotel, Victor Harbor. We had to say I was nineteen as I had been drinking there a few times already, so the barman thought I was 18 already. I loved my life and was looking forward to beginning my training at the next intake now I had turned 17. Before I was due to start, literally two weeks away, my nana and the Matron had a conversation with my mother. Mum had convinced them that I needed to home to NSW. I had no idea about this until Matron summoned to her office. I honestly, hand to heart believed she was going to give me my start date for the PTS nurses training. I was surprised to see nana and grandpa sitting in her office. I then thought they, as guardians may need to sign some documents. The butterflies were there, so excited. Matron started the proceedings off by advising me that my mother had spoken to her re my welfare and mentioned my mother was unwell. She had recently been hospitalized. I was required to return to NSW as soon as possible.

My mind went blank. My vision was blurred I felt like I was going to faint right there I front of Matron. Feeling like I had been swallowed into a black hole. NO NO please don't make me leave! Begging both grandparents and Matron. Regrettably mum had convince them all that she was seriously ill and I was needed to care for my two younger siblings. An urgent call to my dad to beg him to let me stay and complete my nursing training. He said it was my mother's request, but he would be pleased to have me home. I had to process this in my head, I did not want to leave. Dad tried to persuade me with things like,

"I can look into some nursing positions and training for you, somewhere local".

With a heavy heart and full of anger and disappointment two weeks later I returned home. Dad once again met me at Oak Flats station. Being very despondent for weeks didn't help my mood. It was good to see all my siblings and we had lots to talk about. Seeing mum with no dire strait major medical condition, made me more annoyed. Mum had been on Ward 20 which was the psychiatric unit. She had MDD. Major Depressive Disorder. Well, I thought, haven't we all? I did not know what this really meant back in those days. Since then I have completed postgraduate studies in this area, so I understand a lot more.

The Nurses Board of NSW only had its board meetings every six months. So I needed to wait for their 'approval' to start my training. Nursing was extremely hard to get into in the early 70's. I managed to get employed by a hospital in Auburn NSW. Would you believe it, run by nuns! At least I could live in the nurses' Quarters. I had learnt lots of skills and attended as many seminars as I could, so I never had any problem getting employed in a hospital. The nurses' living quarters comprised three levels and a very large swimming pool. On hot study (Theory) days we were allowed to sit around the pool to study. That in fact was the only good thing I can recall. At some point the nurse's quarters required repainting. As they completed one floor at a time, second floor nurses temporarily moved to any spare rooms on level three, and first level occupied vacant rooms on level two. As there were six rooms required for six first floor occupants, these six nurses went to the convent and lived with the nuns. Guess who got picked. Yes, I was one of the six chosen. Lucky me!

Taking only the necessities, nightwear, toiletries such as soap toothbrush etc., is very limited. There were no mirrors, no air conditioning, and only one small window behind the bed. On the back of the bedroom door, there was a small notice on the fire exit plan and a huge Crucifix which was rather daunting. As if Jesus was watching you all night. For six nights, that's all, six long nights in this nunnery. Will I survive? On the fourth night about 2am I felt the room shake… or did I? At first I thought it was that Crucifix falling off the door. No, maybe it was God being angry with me for some reason. In any event, when I went on duty I was informed we had endured an earthquake and many areas around Sydney felt it. Phew that was a relief. The other student nurses living in the convent with me thought they were being punished by God for evil thoughts. We laughed about that for weeks. At St. Joseph's Hospital I had my first insight into class distinction, judgmental and discrimination which led to workplace bullying. I just didn't know it at that stage of my career. These days is runs rampant despite so many laws against it and legislations. Perhaps it should have been nipped in the bud in the 70's and return of the Matrons, or was she the start of it?

During my nursing CarerI have seen many changes, the main one was educating student nurses in universities in Australia. In

1985 in NSW changed from hospital training to university undergraduate degree. In the early 1990's all states changed. (History of Nursing. Nursing in Australia – Wikipedia) Nurse Assistants were no longer employed leaving a gap in the ratio of staff to patients. The student nurses from the universities were expected to do unpaid clinical practical experience in a hospital setting or some other institution as a nursing home, community health centers to achieve skills to get ticked off. Was it practical training? Was it just turning up and getting things ticked off your 'to-do list'? I questioned it was the best experience to give you the best skills? Did they really want to be skilled in that particular area of health, or just going through the motions? In the hospital training days, I enjoyed the hands-on upskilling, most of the higher-level nurses would have the patience and better time management to actually teach me without derogatory remarks or criticism.

Having been through both types of nursing education I feel qualified to have an opinion on today's learning. Too much Industrial and Government input. Interestingly I became an elected Australian Nursing Federation member and Representative and Conference Delegate. I trained in Industrial Relations, learning about ambits and fighting with other reps and members to get changes to policies changed, pay rates increased, and accepted. Somehow twenty years later there were nurses and union reps still fighting for rights or ambits that were offered up as in place of something else. I do not recall ever agreeing to give up something we had fought for and won, in an industrial forum to lose it as an offering up for another ambit. It did not make sense to me at all. Nurse Unions seemed to be going in the wrong direction. Now, we have hospitals employing student nurses from universities as nurse assistants, or called by some other degrading title. They work for cheaper rates to fill todays void in the nurse-to-patient ratio. Plus, these 'nurse assistants' are still required to attend Clinical Placements for the universities without pay! Go figure, no wonder it's a mess in health, financially, and educationally.

STOP, REASSESS and LOOK. The hospitals are having financial issues, nursing staff retention issues and there never seems to be enough beds for those who need them. The outpatient waiting list are so long and it just goes on and on. You almost need to be on death's door to get into Emergency Departments' beds just to get assessed by triage. To get admitted sometimes takes ages and several doctors to decide if you actually need the bed, or send you home to come back later! I recall waiting in an Emergency Department as a patient, sent there from another hospital via ambulance with IV antibiotics running at the time. Once I arrived at the receiving major hospital I was offered a dining chair in an alcove in an office in a corridor. I waited till a specialized ENT team arrived. It was cold, uncomfortable, and was directly in the way of any access to the Allied Health office. An hour later a team doctor turned up, I had not complained but was very annoyed. Saddened by the fact after over forty years of dedicated nursing I had to endure this treatment. What the hell did I fight for so vigorously during my career?

Looking back on that experience in 2020, I was grateful to be a nurse who had mates and colleagues from the same era and had the same work ethic as I did. Six weeks prior to completing my Bachelor of Nursing degree at the University of Wollongong NSW, I had been working hard to finish my remaining two weeks' clinical practicum and working as an Enrolled Nurse all weekend, as we didn't get paid for Monday to Friday clinical practical! I was absolutely exhausted and did not want to do the extra shifts due to final exams coming up and had a couple of assignment to complete. Long story short, I suffered a stroke! I studied hard, I worked hard, and I had a stroke. Yes, indeed the nurse had become the patient. Thankfully I ended up in the Emergency Department where the nursing staff knew me. I presented with a letter from my GP, who was NO help at all. His diagnosis of me was that nothing was wrong with me. Later after recovering I took him to the Health Commission's Complaints Department. Still have all the documentation on that case!

The staff at Wollongong Hospital were absolutely fantastic in my recovery from the stroke. Receiving the best care from skilled nurses, the best Neurologist Specialist in the state, top Cardiologist,

Endocrinologist, and the entire team ensured I survived. Despite the fact I couldn't talk properly my nursing mates understood me very well and helped in my recovery. My daughter was called, not sure if I called her or the hospital, but I remember seeing her with her husband. I clearly remember her reaction wasn't positive, am sure she didn't think I was actually unwell and felt like an 'inconvenience'. After being triaged I didn't recall anything, even the CT scan I had been given. I do remember having an ECG in a private room at the end of the Emergency Department. I knew the nurses who were looking after me, but I was just not sure of their names back then. Felt I was slipping in and out of consciousness. My family visited me but the conversations were all a blur. Their voices I could hear, but I was unable to respond, in my head I was talking but nothing was coming out. My dreams were blurry and hard to distinguish what was real and what wasn't for a while.

My nursing mates were there most of the time which was very calming for me. Some were actually working on the C4 ward and saw me on every shift. The Neurologist required an MRI. Well that would be a firm NO from me, that's definitely not happening, claustrophobia my greatest fear. Then with a wave of the hand, the specialist ordered an injection of Valium, and next thing I knew my friend, the nurse, injected me, within a few minutes I was on my way to have the MRI. The guy in the scrubs asked me about music, what would I like.... Robbie Williams I recall in my head, but apparently out like a light before I even began to get onto the MRI bed. Just as well I know I wouldn't have made it without smashing something. A piece of equipment, someone's face …. Ha-ha! Now this happened twice in one week. The Neurologist required another spinal check as he needed to check if I had MS.

"No way, you had one shot at it. No no!" again with a wave of the hand but two fingers displayed, yes, I got a double shot. I don't recall leaving the ward, let alone going through any MRI! I was in my bed attached to a BP cuff, the nurse informed me the MRI had been done and I immediately fell back to sleep until teatime.

After two weeks and unbearable physiotherapy, being very painful and exhausting work, but I was forced to participate by the till of the Hun. The first time I could walk those bars unassisted, I got dressed, walked sneakily past the nurse's station, proceeded down the lift and out onto the street. The coffee shop was nearby in Crown St. I ordered a magnificent medium cappuccino with two sugars and snuck back to my ward. The young lady in the bed next to me laughed when she saw me sneak in. She was so nice, about 30 years, diagnosed with Raynaud's Syndrome, and was constantly feeling numb and cold. She went for investigations in theatre a few days later, we were both in the Day Surgery holding area. I was having an endoscopy for the first time. She never came back. She has died from inoperable cancer. Gosh it was so sad. The last night we were in the ward together we placed a sheet over the over way table, pinched a small vase with a rose in it and dined together looking out at the night view of Crown Street. That was her last meal, a Bittersweet memory. I was glad to be alive. I was later discharged to my daughters' as the Rehabilitation Unit had been struck down with gastro.

Recovering from a stroke isn't easy. Your legs need to move by concentrating from the brain to tell your legs to actually move. It felt like you are walking in deep snow, every step was an effort just to lift and move forward. Every step is in slow motion. Even thinking and talking were slow. Some things were missing from memory and conversation. It certainly took me a long time and lots of medical assistance. My rehabilitation case manager was so wonderful at the Commonwealth Rehabilitation Services. She not only monitored my general health but also my mental health. She understood the emotional support required. When I had specialist appointments or physiotherapy Renee always accompanied me. The hand therapy was the most painful and during these appointments I received two cortisone injections, which were an absolute bitch and painful. Unfortunately required more years later for the same issue, tenosynovitis.

Eventually I recovered bit by bit. I lost a lot during the process, family and some friends. That is however another story! As I mentioned I still had to complete my nursing degree with some exams and a couple of clinical practical's. I did, it wasn't easy as a lot was going on in my life and family issues. However, my brother Tom was on my side. It was a happy day for me. I had to start a new life, working with fellow new graduates in Mental Health, Julie, Anne Maree and a few others who all worked together and new friendships were formed. We all completed our post graduate studies in Mental Health Nursing (which I graduated with a credit!)We all went on to do out Masters in Mental Health Nursing in 2009.

I thought Mental Health was interesting and put everything into it. I had learnt so much from my peers and tutors, Jennifer, Mark and Terry. Not to forget the incredible Phillip, who had an obsession with Brittany Spears back in the day. We were sure to get a good pass if you added a picture of her in your power point presentation! Did I mention he gave me a Credit! So now I was in full time employment post the stroke in 2006, so it was 2009 not bad for a 3-year hiatus. Thank goodness the Nurses Board of NSW did have anything to say regards my 'break' in training. I have definitely had to do the hard yards over the years with theory and practical in nursing. To be perfectly honest I missed being an Enrolled nurse once I became a Registered nurse. But I worked extremely hard to upskill at every opportunity and enjoyed being a Clinical Nurse and then a Nursing Manager in top clinical roles in many jobs. Working in three Australian states, NSW, SA and Vic., gave me a variety of nursing positions and with everyone I gave 100%.

Back in nursing lifestyle again it was good for everything, financially, and plenty opportunities to get out and enjoy life. Anne –Maree graduated together and we began working together in Mental Health Inpatient Units. We were elevated to the sharing role as Nurse Unit Manager during a few changes of NUM's. We had a great working relationship and a good friendship. One of our nursing colleagues, Anne, who everyone affectionately called 'mother', more like a Matron, unfortunately passed away in 2023. Another 'old school' nurse and brilliant at her job. Definitely kept the newbies on their feet. She was very fair and firm with the patients too! Not much got passed her either. Of course I was elected OH&S representative along with the Wards man / Security, Derek, known as our HASA. We are still mates too after years of friendship. He is an amazing man. We live in different states now but caught up with him and his wife a couple of years ago in South Australia.

In 2009 four of us nurses plus two other friends booked a Corporate package to attend the Melbourne Cup Spring Festival. Over $2000.00! Anne –Maree, Julie, her sister Lesley and her best friend, Rhonda all booked this trip, I was so excited as it was around my birthday time. Another nurse, Karen decided to come along too at the last minute, all six of us were ecstatic about flying over, the Travel Lodge Motel rooms and all the fun at the race days! I thought it would be awesome to take my granddaughter, Imogen to the Melbourne Cup one year. She had always loved horses and had her own until she had a severe accident on one of her horses. The Melbourne Cup trip was absolutely so much fun and would like to do that again. Maybe something different like go to Paris or London. We paired up into our allocated rooms. Anne – Maree and I had two double beds, the room was awesome and didn't take us long to fill the room with chaos by littering the floor in bedroom and the bathroom too! The bed area quickly became a jumble of clothes, shoes and underwear.

Leslie and Rhonda shared a room and were most civilized ones of all. Julie and Karen shared the third room. Not sure if that was a good idea, but someone had to do it. The first morning of the Corporate Sportsnetfour day fiesta was the 'Special Sportsnet Breakfast' at the Eureka Tower next door. This was a horrifying shock to me due to my claustrophobia. 83 floors high, one small lift, well it felt small to me. Lots of guests in this one lift with us. I was hyperventilating, eyes shut tight, five women holding on to me, chanting,

"We are nearly there, breathe …. breathe …." Not only could I hear them, I could hear the recorded voice saying what floor we were on (39th), how fast we were travelling. OMG I almost fainted. Thank God my colleagues were holding me close. The girls were laughing their heads off and trying to comfort me at the same time. Once we arrived at the top floor, pretty sure it was the top, I literally flew out the elevator knocking people out of my way! Holy

Shit! I was greeted by a huge room surrounded by glass walls, windows for walls. Think I may have wet myself LOL. After the traumatic entrance and I settled down to a normal breathing pattern, I managed to sit at our reserved table to welcome a very fancy breakfast. We were offered some Champagne by some very hot waiters.

"Well thank you, just what I needed". Despite it was only 9.15am. The breakfast was absolutely a delicious feast.

The finest foods, eggs cooked in every way possible, gourmet sausages, bacon with fruit of every kind in season and exquisite range of yogurts. So much to choose from, actually felt like Julia Roberts in 'Pretty Woman'. We were clinking champagne flutes, laughing and having the best time ever. I spotted the Caviar and unashameably made a bee line for it. My first encounter with Caviar was at an Oncology Conference event in Sydney where the Oncology Specialists paid for us Oncology nurses a table of ten. It costs $100 each. I turned up my nose at the stuff at first and asked one on the nurses,

"What is that? It looks disgusting." The waiter leaned over and whispered in my ear,

"That is the most expensive delicacy on the table." He smiled and with a small silver spoon he offered me to taste it. I did.

I loved it. I then devoured every little pot I found on the tables. I have had a love affair ever since.

After eating and drinking at the Corporate Breakfast it came time to go to the bathroom. Luckily a couple of the girls came with me. Shock of horrors, all glass walls in 360 degrees' view of Melbourne. I felt so dizzy and leaned against the wall of glass, grabbing the marble vanity and uttered something like 'Shit'… The actual toilets were surrounded by beautiful wooden doors and walls. It felt good to just sit there on the loo without having to look out a window to freak me out. Eventually I came out, and used the luxurious silky soft hand wash and was brave enough to take some photos of this 360 degree view, as I knew I was never going to see it again! So after my heart had stopped pounding I managed to catch up with my mates who weren't just nurses, they were Mental Health nurses and tried not to laugh at my emotional rollercoaster. They did extremely well not to laugh, well not while I was around. We continued to attend the race days leading up to the Melbourne Cup 2009, the 149th running of the Thoroughbred horses. Julie had a 2nd on Crime Scene which was beaten by Shocking. None of the rest of us even got close. Surprisingly I met Bart Cummings, such a lovely man.

We attended Derby Day with all the Celebrities and A liters. Oaks Day was Ladies Day, on the Thursday after the Cup, Stakes Day was family day with all the fashions and dress codes. One of these nights at the Travel Lodge some of the girls wanted to see 'This Is It', the late Michael Jacksons movie playing not too far from our motel. As I had a surprised phone call from a friend of mine, Brett, who quite by chance was staying in a nearby Motel. So guess what? I didn't go with the girls. Brett was on a business trip; I took a taxi to his motel. Feeling very much like Julia Roberts again as he met me in the luxurious Foyer, he escorted me to the Piano Bar sitting in the soft leather chairs that felt like soft clouds on the back of my bare legs. My little black dress showed off my recently spray tanned legs that Anne – Maree's daughter treated me before we flew out. Complete with slim black stiletto heels to enhance the look of long legs. Despite that fact I was only 5 feet 2 inches. Not long after our 'hello' alcoholic drinks, we ventured up to glamourous suite. The views were incredible from the long windows in the suite. I didn't feel sick or giddy in the elevator coming up or even looking at the views from up high. No claustrophobia, just relaxed and pampered. Brett and I had met about a year ago and our 'Friends with Benefits' was working out quite well. We would usually meet up at my unit or somewhere in Sydney and go out to a fancy restaurant for lunch. Normally our visits would last up to three hours, quality mixed with quantity. This was the first time we had both been in Melbourne at the same time, it was so romantic, especially when we didn't plan it.

This was also our first nighttime Rendezvous as day time was easier. This was special for us, more than just French Champagne, cheese platters and fantastic views. Very much like a dream date. Unfortunately he had to fly back to Sydney early in the morning and I had a big day of shopping with the girls around Melbourne's Fashion District. By midnight I was in a taxi returning to my own Motel. Yes, all the girls were waiting and gave me a hard time, and all the next day. I just laughed, and they said they were just jealous. The shopping expedition in Melbourne's most elite stores was fabulous and we bought so much we had trouble fitting it into our suitcases. The 54cm Eiffel Tower just managed to fit into my suitcase. I had to give away a 6 pack of beer the day we booked out, some young guys were checking in as we were checking out. They couldn't believe their luck. As Karen, Lesley and Rhonda had left the day earlier it was just us three to run amuck in the city before our flight back to Sydney. I was looking forward to sleeping in my own bed.

Chapter 7:
Returning to Reality.

Not sure how long it was after returning home from our awesome time away, but I felt different. I had such a great relaxed and fun time away, but now I felt deflated and depressed. I had started seeing a mate, Mark, who had always had a thing for me, infatuated perhaps. As it turns out he was a player, and not a good one. The girls at work would laugh when I would say After work,

"Just going out for some coffee and cake." Most of them quickly worked out that 'cake' was not a bakery item. One of my friends who had a son by him, by accident, an accidental donor perhaps, in any case she was pregnant by a guy she had met and started dating who was related to Mark's ex-wife's boyfriend. It was all very confusing but we all got along, we just kept things to ourselves. Mistake no. 1. It gets worse and more complicated. There was a birthday party for their son. Rachelle and Mark's son that is. I was invited by Rachelle as we were friends. All her friends and family went. She had four sisters, no brothers. Only one of them I didn't trust. There is always one in the crowd and this chick was trouble, but Rachelle couldn't see it and I tried to tell her…

"But she's my sister." She would always say in a real winey pitiful way. So annoying and so gullible. I actually would say she was more vulnerable and people would take advantage of her naivety.

At the party the kids were playing Ten Pin Bowling and having a great time. I noticed one of Rachelle's sisters let's call her miss B, flirting opening with Mark. I had this cramp in my belly like something foreboding was going to happen. It was totally inappropriate and something wasn't right. My body was always right with this kind of thing. I had been through a heartbreaking divorce in 1996 that I haven't disclosed yet, but my gut was telling me something wasn't right. By golly I was right! Over ten years of heartbreak, therapy and months of dark days and thoughts of suicide to get where I was in my soul. During this time, I was studying the rest of my Masters in Mental Health Nursing. I was feeling overwhelmed during these months with assignments and was feeling depressed. I began to close off to friends and family, especially my work colleagues who I shared everything. I felt like this had something to do with Mark, so I decided to face him and clear the air and confront him. No he wasn't seeing anyone else,

"You are definitely all I need. The questions kept going and his answers always the same. But that feeling was still as strong as ever. Always a sign, never fails me. Believe me I wish I didn't have it, but my body senses these things. One afternoon Rachelle began getting some intermittent contractions so we all decided to meet at Marks' place to put a strategy in place for when she goes into hospital for baby No. 3. As she had the two boys we planned the babysitting, well Mark was having son No 2 as his father. She went to hospital and Mark and I went in to visit her as a couple. That was an extraordinary day! However she was sent home for a few days as midwife says she no quite in labor yet. Ok, so as a good friend I offered to stay with her a few nights as I was the only medical person amongst them.

Somehow we get invited over to Mark's house for dinner, he was preparing some nice dish of something. Don't recall because all hell broke loose that day! As I have said, Mark was a player, just not a smart one. The dad of baby N0.3 had some disability, like Asperger's or something, but he definitely not a player. Turns out there was an argument the two guys regard to a paternity test. Say What! Mark insisted the baby was his. How could that be? I had been seeing him for past eight months. Turns out the paternity test proved that Mark was not the father of baby No. 3., so Mark thinks oh everything is ok then and all is forgiven and forgotten! No way and no more cake for him! Rachelle and I had a huge fight. The real baby daddy was fed up with all this but not quite smart enough to do anything about the situation. Me? I felt totally betrayed by both of them, Mark and Rachelle.

Two months after the baby was born, we bumped into each other at the local shopping center, we spoke a few pleasantries and for some stupid reason I agreed to meet up with her at Mark's for lunch. This really only came about as Mark had been phoning me constantly at home and at my workplace to forgive him. Of course he promised all the bullshit that guys say when they have been caught out cheating. Strike two! We were all sitting around the dining table, Rachelle had just finished breast feeding the bubs, another boy, when the phone rang. After a very brief conversation Mark hands the phone to Rachelle, looking very pale and after another brief chat, Rachelle hands the phone back to Mark. I really didn't think much of it and just started setting the table for three. The caller was her eldest sister, married to a Maori guy. I had met them both several times at family functions, nice people. OH well here's the kicker! Apparently the youngest sister, the one I didn't like, don't like, you could go as far as detested, the one from the Ten Pin Bowling birthday bash, yep same bitch, well my gut instincts were correct!

She had 'discovered' quite enthusiastically I may add, to be pregnant. She already had two lovely girls, her husband had committed suicide about a year ago. She was paid a good some from insurance, which Mark and his mates were only too happy to tell her how to spend it. So shock of all shocks she had been sleeping with the eldest sister's husband, but also with Mark! The great conversation was, if it is black its Jade's, if it was white its Marks'. Everyone thought that was simple solution and during the entire pregnancy none of her sisters would speak to her. To my shock both Mark and Jade were hoping to be the father! Even though they had no idea about each other, but am sure guys are strange, dumb or both. I personally wanted to punch her face in. I honestly ready did want to hurt her, she is so lucky it's just not in my DNA.

To my surprise or annoyance Mark still wanted to see me and begged me to forgive him. In the same breath he wanted to 'care' for the 'Bitch' as I called her. I was way beyond hurt and angry. I was a true Scorpion like Mark but I was faithful. My depression turned into helplessness and my disappointment imploded. I was dealing with other issues at the time such as not being able to see my grandchildren anymore, as my estranged daughter moved to Old. I was totally gutted, had been recovering from a stroke five months previous, so I was devoid of any feelings. Had lost interest in work, retreated from those around me. I just didn't see it and neither did any of my work colleagues, even the highly skilled mental health nurse workmates. I was trying to keep myself together. At the same time, I was dealing with an unexpected visit from my niece who I hadn't seen since she was a baby. Now she was grown up, well sixteen anyway. My mum wanted to reunite with her son, my brother, the nieces' father. He did not and I got caught in the middle of a tragic family argument. I was once again disowned 'temporarily' by my mum and youngest sister. So actually I was going through a lot back then.

Both sons were getting married that year, the youngest in Victoria March 2010 and the eldest in Queensland in October 2010. This is what kept me from going over the top, or under, whatever. I had money saved and tried to purchase an apartment opposite the lake at Warilla where l grew up. I am not sure what happened but I didn't get approved due to some bank BS. I cried many nights and work seemed harder. Not knowing what to do I fell in the deep end. The only one supporting me was my brother Tom. So here I was, returned to the Illawarra for ten years and felt I had got nowhere. Ended up with no one, no grandchildren around me anymore. My best friend had married my cousin and now we were all estranged. I spent my days off work at the cemetery sitting beside my nana Crosbie's grave, asking her to help me. Many times I sat there, I cried as I thought about my last marriage. I was so happy then and loved the life and being mum to all the six children. Suddenly it was gone in a flash. I never broke my vows, it was the hardest thing to go through and missing those children that I was forbidden to see after a while. I was so depressed and shocked. I absolutely loved him so much. The emptiness I was feeling then is how it was back then. It is a story to tell another time. Ten years of therapy to get over it, or did I? Things were black and I certainly was in a dark space.

I asked my brother Tom did he need me up near him with his young sons, as he was going through a rough situation with his ex-wife. No he was ok; the boys were ok. I asked my eldest son if I should come up to Queensland, but he was doing very well and was getting married to a wonderful woman, kids were great. My daughter lived up there too, I knew that no way would she want me living up there that close. I still feel this way after I retired from nursing and moved up to my eldest sons'. I hope that before I die all my three of my children love my as much as I love them. There were huge bushfires in Victoria and all the flowers and buildings burnt down on the property where my youngest son was getting married in Sth. Gippsland area. My youngest son was having mental health issues post trauma to the bushfires. Everyone in the area was terrified, some even lost homes, animals it was a terrifying time for all affected. I contacted the local Mental Health Community Team to enquire if there were any vacancies as many people needed support. I spoke with the Community MH person in charge and he requested my CV to be emailed directly to him. I sent it feeling extremely confident. I only had two more subjects to complete my Masters in Nursing Mental Health, and was assured that there would my no problem completing them at La Trobe University on site.

This gave me hope and on the premise of a new life and at the same time seem to procrastinate over it. So during this time the 'Bitch' had her baby, a white boy and the paternity award once again goes to Mark! He had the audacity to come to my door to tell me, to gloat or feel ashamed. Either way had no good emotional attachment to him, to her or the baby! I rang my youngest son to let him know I was moving near him prior to his wedding in March. Tears ran down my face, cramps started again in my gut, I don't remember Mark leaving or even what was said. It was over. Everything went black. Next day I informed my boss, who had taken over the role as NUM making it a total boys' club. After that, the only female nurses that were shown and favoritism were the ones sleeping with them. I can say that absolutely for it was true facts. There were a few pregnancies too just quietly. To hell with the lot of them, I had $12K in the bank and this would help me set up in Gippsland. A new era, new job and near my son. No interests in any type of relationships, ever! So I gave my notice to my boss. He quickly realized he just didn't need to replace a full time RN Clinician with skills and experience as an acting Nurse Unit Manager, I was so much more than that. I was the Depot nurse, OH&S representative, nurse union representative and Conference Delegate, plus the Project Analysis Officer for all the Health Area Stats and the Education Trainer in Mental Health! So good luck with that!!

I organised a removalist to store my furniture and organized another company to store and move certain items to the new residence in Victoria. I had the money and I used it. On the way to Gippsland I called in to visit my niece and brother in Frankston, the one I never grew up with during my childhood. We had a few nights together, some take away dinners and lazy days on the beach. I drove to South Gippsland and booked into my new cabin. It was so handy right next door to the Hospital on one side and on the other was the Airfield. I had missed hear planes flying around from Williamstown RAAF base, living with my ex No. 3. I did not realize till later that I was so close to the Sale RAAF base. It still is too hard to talk about my ex just yet. He had removed any butterflies in my life. Just darkness and a deep hole I was struggling to get out of for years. However, if I had known or someone in my 'friends' circle had of told me, I would have definitely made the effort to see those children. It broke my heart so much. Fortunately one of my step daughters contacted me one new year's eve and we met up for a heartwarming, soul healing catch up. Best New Year Ever, and we've kept in contact ever since.

Moving to Traralgon probably was a mistake. But I did get to spend time with my youngest son. Trying to heal both our hearts was not as easy as I hoped. I lost a bit of my savings until I could get employment. The Community Mental Health Services did not honor the job offer and kept ghosting me at arranged interviews. Very bad PR for sure. Hope they didn't treat their clients like that. I was feeling dark again, like earlier in my life, lost, lonely and scared with foreboding cramps. I was an orphan of the soul. The caretakers at the Village Caravan Park were absolutely wonderful people. I wasn't too far from the shopping center as I had my Ford Fairmont car, black with tinted windows, was a great car. My son and his then wife were only about ten minutes away by car and his father and his wife lived only ten minutes on the other side of town. His wife was very nice to me and I thought she was a good person.

After presenting myself to the CMH to try and catch up with 'Graeme' who was never available even after several promises and to this day I have never met him. Becoming very depressed at this point with only two modules left for my Master's Degree and no employment in Mental Health to complete it, I was very upset, disappointed and financially ruined. It cost me $1500.00 to get half my furniture to get delivered, and $1500.00 to pack remove and store furniture in NSW. I paid in advance to put Bond and advanced rent on the cabin, before I drove all the way from Warilla to Traralgon. So I had paid all this hard earned money to relocate to this freezing cold and so far lonely place. My youngest son was studying to get into the Victorian Police Force as he wasn't very happy with his current job. He wanted to get ahead in life. Guess he was feeling the same as myself. He did seem very popular with his team at work, but you need to do what you need to do. After a break up with a girlfriend, who I did like, it wasn't long before another girl had her eyes on him. A bit too soon I thought, but that's just a mothers' opinion... I didn't listen to my mum either. But when you're young you get to make mistakes. As it turned out, the first one broke his heart, the second one financially ruined him, unfortunately they married and were together for years. I will never forget her mother saying to me,

"She could have had anyone but she wanted to have Michael!" and this was said on their wedding day. I was so appalled by her remark it burned into my memory forever.

There had apparently been some issue with the bridesmaids and six weeks before the wedding new ones were arranged. By the time I had found out it was too late, the cauldron was already full of witch's brew, actually 'bitches brew.' How do you deal with that sort of nonsense? I really wanted to tell his father and his wife but what could we do collectively? The mother having the gall to say that to your face with no remorse. As it turned out she was a bit on the side of crazy. More like bipolar and now my daughter in law was showing signs of this too. The brother also had issues but not like those two with a touch of crazy traits. The husband also was ruined financially by their massive spending traits. Thank goodness he had the smarts to protect himself and his possessions. Looking back on 5 years of marriage to my son, he realized his daughter was in over her head. Nobody won, everybody lost except the father. The jury isn't out on how I feel about him yet, 9 years later. At the time I was employed and if she earned $100 in her job, she would spend $500. Most weeks after I started working again she would ask me to 'help' her out financially, but not to mention it to my son. I never said anything until after they were divorced. I had kept every receipt from the bank, $500 here, $300 there. She never ever paid me back. But I have to proof in bank statements.

As I wasn't working for a few weeks when I first moved, and before I had any interviews, my mate Julie the nurse from NSW that went to the Melbourne Cup trip with me, came to visit me in my little cabin. I had set my cabin up in a nice style. Using the blue sofa bed as the spare bed for Julie, the fridge was a godsend as I had insulins that needed to be kept cold. My queen size bed and mattress with two bedside drawers fitted just perfectly into the bedroom. The wardrobes were built in with sliding doors. The main issue I had was it was a pay as you go metered electricity coin box, which took 20 cent pieces so using $1.20 per day on average. As I was then still unemployed and Centrelink weren't paying me anything, not even a concession card for medications, times were very tough for me. I mean really tough and this led to increased depression, enduring very cold dark nights and needing to keep my insulin in a small sky inside the fridge without power. My washing I had to do by hand in an old trough in the communal laundry as I had no coins to use the washing machines. In Gippsland the winters were extremely icy cold. Many nights I would lay in bed in the dark with layers of blankets, coats and clothes. Crying myself to sleep.

The worst was no food or power to even make a hot drink. These were days of doom. I wandered around the caravan park during the day seeking a stray 20 cent piece or two, and that's when I discover the camp kitchen! What luck indeed, it was very basic but it had a kettle, toaster and a little fridge. But best of all it had power! I ran as fast as I could back to my cabin and scrummaged through my barren pantry for a teabag. Yes, I had two, plus about 30mls of milk left. Running back to the camp kitchen, turned the kettle on and enjoyed the best cup of tea in ages. I realized I needed to get some food due to my diabetes rather than my hunger pains. The next day I went to the Salvation Army store to ask if there was an office to assist with food. The lady explained you needed to make an appointment and would need to fit the criteria. I burst into tears, big sobbing tears, unrelenting, embarrassed and unashamed. Collapsing into a chair I covered my face, saying nothing as I had nothing to say. Two very stout ladies came from nowhere to my aid. It took me a few minutes before I could speak. I babbled my story of woe, not sure if anyone understood me. It was one of my worst days of my life. In my head I was praying

"Lord take me now, please." It was about an hour later when I realized I was in a different room altogether. One lady beside me, holding my hand and the other lady was quickly filling up plastic bags with bread, bread rolls, tins of fruit and tinned food and bags of pasta. One lady handed me a $30 food voucher and $10 worth of 20cent coins.

My pride was crushed but my belly was full. I was able to have a hot shower that night! First hot shower in three days. No electricity and no hot water for 3 days. How ashamed I was to think I left it all for this. I did sleep well that night. Being so thankful to those ladies. There were many incidents like this for a long while. Too embarrassed to ask for help. Two weeks later I got a job interview at Sale District Community Nursing. Not exactly what I wanted but hey I needed a job. So good news I did get the job as RN at Sale District Community Nursing. I slept well and the next day invited my son and daughter in law over for tea. It was a grand feast and we celebrated my finally getting a job. As per usual Centrelink had just granted me my concession card and new start, whatever it was called then. After being unemployed for 6 weeks, no income at all and had to use every cent of my savings. Whoa, I just could believe it, Centrelink cancelled my money as I was now employed, despite the fact I hadn't even earnt anything or started yet! I was so angry at the system. Centrelink almost sent me over the edge and down a very dark path.

I had enough money for 2 weeks rent, but nothing for petrol to get there and back for 2 weeks. In desperation I asked my friend Julie for a loan for petrol and explain about the job. Without any questions she deposited the $100 into my bank. I repaid her when I got paid. So very grateful to Julie. As I had a few 5 cent pieces in a jar, I asked the elderly lady in the next cabin if I could swap them for 20-cent pieces. What a life saver she was, she gave me some extra coins so I could have a shower. I must admit I had become very frugal with money. Money I didn't have, such as using the camp kitchen kettle and toaster, I save money by watching TV in the recreation room until it closed at 9pm. I found a magazine one day in the TV room which had a Mother's Day card in it. I tore it out, wrote on it, and posted it to my mother in South Australia. She absolutely was thrilled with it, but I never told her the story behind it, maybe one day I will tell her. She would understand and love it more.

It was extremely hard making friends, except my ex's new wife, she was very good to me and included me in all the family gatherings. I never told her of my struggles prior to getting employment at Sale. As I mentioned before the staff were mostly nice and friendly. I upskilled any nursing areas that I needed in my scope of practice. Undertaking an update course in venipuncture as the RN in a regional – rural you definitely need these skills. The same for palliative care, I upskilled and specialized in this area with specific dressing and changing PICC lines,(Peripherally Inserted Central Catheter) Which is a type of long catheter inserted through a peripheral vein, usually in an arm, into a larger vein in the body. The PICC line had to be in place for long term medications like Chemotherapy. Only a trained, experienced nurse could change the outer dressing. Extremely Aseptic technique and

Cytotoxictechnique required. I really enjoyed doing those and was always a self-disciplined nurse when it came to Aseptic procedures and wound care. There wasn't much I couldn't do with helping with all cancer patients, including Chemotherapy and Nikki pumps.

Over time the patients and their families trusted me with their 'at home' medical equipment, CADD machines, IV antibiotics, Kidney Dialysis care. I still was a firm believer and advocate for Nikki pumps and using various medications such as morphine, Atropine and Midazolam. There were so many wound care products for specific healing such as products to assist in closing up post-surgical wounds. One of my patients out there in the regional area had open heart surgery and was recovering at home. His surgical wound wasn't closing properly so the District Nursing Services took over the care. I could see right inside his chest cavity, and see the chambers of his heart beating. Definitely an aseptic process. We monitored healing, preventing inflammation and infections, using specific wound care products, medications and even diet. I was always amazed at watching the skin growing and healing. The wound was just a huge gaping hole that gradually became smaller on the inside to a small manageable scar on the outside. You know then you have done a wonderful job as a nurse.

Over the years I have received letters and cards from patients and families thanking me for helping them in their darkest hours. Some grandparents and parents of celebrities, and some were

133

everyday people who had a severe medical or surgical condition and were very thankful for my services. Sometimes I would get a call out late at night from patients or family members suffering breakthrough pain, requiring more morphine to help them. No matter how remote they lived or in a stormy night or how late the hour was, I always would go to them. I was authorized to draw up more syringes of morphine, capped and leave for the next breakthrough pain. It was just as relieving for the family as it was for the patient. Most of the cancer patients I knew very well, including their doctors and oncologists, and every medication. The continuity of care was so necessary in regional and remote areas. They knew I was only a call away. There were three main hospitals that I mainly worked with when out and about during my workday. If I had a call from my boss regards to a 'chemo client' having an urgent medical situation, I would contact one of these smaller rural hospitals to collect cytotoxic PPE or Chemotherapy they would have it ready for me to collect. They all knew me well. My vehicle was equivalent to an ambulance. I took pride in being reliable to those suffering at home.

My mum became ill in South Australia and long story short I drove back and forth every fortnight using my sick leave and then annual leave, eventually I had to relocate to SA. My son and daughter in law eventually had a beautiful son. Unfortunately, her spending became worse, nothing for the baby. All high-end items for herself. She rang me one night begging to borrow some money.

"I definitely repay you when I go back to work, we'll work out a plan…" So I lent her $5000! Later on I paid her credit card off and her car registration. Amazing she never ever paid me back. They eventually broke up, she stopped me from seeing my grandson and my rage within carried over for many years. Luckily I kept all receipts from the bank transfers. She took the money and the baby and ran to mummy. Karma I felt got both of them when they all got kicked out of the beautiful property when her dad began a relationship with the mothers' friend. They all lived happily ever after, as far as I know or care. I lost my grandson in the process. One day I will turn up on her doorstep, I know where she lives!

My son was depressed, angry and lost. Before he had time to get himself together, another young lady was waiting in the wings! They dated for a while, broke up but just as he was getting his life in order, she announces she's pregnant. So another merry go round. She was a beautiful little girl, named after my mother. I visited them every month, bought her things from London and Paris when I went overseas a month after she was born. She is such a delight. The parents broke up. I continued to visit my granddaughter until the mother forbade me! No reason just stopped communication. I have FaceTime chats when she is with my son. Of course I took her to family court lawyers. After a year it seemed useless, and in anger and frustration I stopped my lawsuit. I get to see her when my son sees her. That's ok for now. She is so much a daddy's girl with my mum's determination and sassy! Absolutely love it. She will please herself when she is older and my door will always be open.

Chapter 8:
Regional Cancers

The range of different cancers and the ages of the patients were astonishing to me. Even after seeing the young deaths at the Bairnsdale Cemetery, times and diseases had changed over a century but so many of my patients were diagnosed with cancer in the South. Gippsland. If I weren't working fulltime and being the on call Palliative care nurse, I would have become an 'Erin Brockovich' and investigated why. Even men were not immune to Breast Cancer! Obviously, I had many female patients with Breast Cancer too, more males with Brain Cancer and all young men with young families. It was heartbreaking to see what they went through. I decided to join the Gippsland Cancer Committee. I was so involved and attended the best Conferences and any workshops and saw some amazing developments in Cancer Research. I was so impressed that I applied for my Master's in Nursing (Breast Cancer). It was a very difficult and complex study but enjoyed it. I received a letter from the 'Jane McGrath Breast Cancer Foundation' stating that I had been chosen for the $10,000 Scholarship for the Breast Cancer Nurse in Gippsland. I was so thrilled and I didn't even apply for any Scholarship. I still have the document today, framed.

Within weeks of receiving the letter, my sister contacted me regarding my mother being in the ICU in a major hospital in SA. Oh buggar, this so reminded me of 1972 when I was about to start my first official training in SA. My son and his wife were over for a Sunday roast, as we often didn't get days off the same. I was enjoying their visit to my new white French-style house, which I was renting off one of the nurses. We shared the house for a while, then she bought another one when she semi-retired. She was going to be a Forensic Clean Nurse. I thought that was awesome. So this is when I drove back and forth to Adelaide, my aunt Gwen, sister Kathy and brother Tom came from all over different states to see mum in the hospital. Mum had often been to that hospital so they knew of her cardiac condition. Her heart was failing and she was on a respirator for quite a while.

Eventually, she was able to breathe on her own and moved to the Private Hospital attached to the major public hospital. She had also been admitted to this hospital previously so they knew of her. All of us siblings were there, checking on mum, talking to nurses, doctors, and social workers. Basically all her medical team. The day came when this doctor came into a room to speak to the three of us, Tom, Margaret, and me. Straight up she says in quite a matter-of-fact manner,

"Your mother is dying and not eating, so we are going to take her off all medication and nil by mouth. The speech therapist has tried but your mother refuses to eat…" She then continues to add in the same matter-of-fact tone, "So she will be dead in a week." She wiped her hands as if gesturing 'and that will be that'. We were all horrified and most upset by this, no way this was going to happen! I waited for the speech therapist to try to feed Mum for the last time. Mum was awake but unable to articulate any words. I said firmly to the therapist than mum will not eat it if she doesn't like the taste. Then I turned to mum, holding her hands tightly, and said,

"You need to eat mum, eat something, if you don't eat anything well that's it, it will be all over!" She was staring straight into my eyes and could see my tears. I took the pureed apple from the therapist, let mum hold it, and tried a small spoonful. She moved her lips to taste it. She liked it. I encouraged her to have more, we continued this pattern and eventually she began eating by herself little bits at a time. I was so happy and my sister informed the nurses including 'Dr Death'. Anyway she improved little by little despite the medical team saying she would never be able to care for herself anymore. We were advised to look for a nursing home for her. Well we did and my sister had plenty of contacts, as a qualified Social Worker, and I as a Registered Nurse knew where not to place her. We had a wonderful agency and after a few weeks in Cardiac Rehabilitation she was offered a few placements. I went back and forth to SA to help as much as I could.

My studies fell short with limited time to complete assignments and exams, I advised the La Trobe University coordinator of the situation and that I needed to relocate to be near my mum. It really saddened me that I had to decline the Jane McGrath Foundation Scholarship. They were understanding and perhaps I could continue in SA. I felt absolutely horrible leaving my youngest son when he was going through his own issues. I wish now that they could have moved into the house in Sale, but it was what it was. Of course every day I would question my leaving since they had their little baby on the way. Funny how life turns a corner and you are completely blind sighted. I kept only a third of my furniture and donated the rest to the Salvos that had helped me when I was unemployed. I needed to ensure I got a job back in Adelaide or I would be in the same position as it was in 2010. I stayed at Glenelg at a backpacker for a few weeks, it wasn't that bad. Eventually I shared a house in Seaford Meadows. Nice place, brand new. Short distance to my sister and short distance from mum. We placed her in a really nice nursing home close to my sisters' house. I spent the days with mum and worked agency in the afternoon. My sister worked and studied in the days and visited mum in the evenings. On the weekends we both would take her out to the shops in a wheelchair. Oh goodness we had some funny times together during that time.

Unfortunately, I still had storage in NSW that I was paying for, I quickly became tired of the storage game. Was also tired of just settling into a place, finding my own space creating a new lifestyle and friends and having to up and leave. I felt sad, lonely and hoped not to get into any financial situation again. No more Salvation Army visits. First thing I had to do was re-join the nursing agency. It was always a pain to change your address for things like Nurses registration, driver's license and things like that. It was what is was, I had to suck it up and get on with it. One great thing about being in Adelaide was seeing my old friends again. Diana was one of them. We ended up working together again at the same place we met. It was so good. The owner moved in with his fiancée near the city and so I had the whole house to myself. I felt queen of the manor. At last I was settled.my family came for gatherings and mum loved it as no stairs. She was pretty good with her wheelie walker, hard to stop her once she got going. Everyone at work came to my place for parties, I had my 60th birthday there. Magic days for sure and I was loving life again. I don't know where I managed to find the time, but I was elected as Secretary and news editor for the Seaford District Residents Association. That kept me busy working along the police with the Neighborhood Watch.

I still was working full time nursing and doing the Manager in Mental Health in country areas. I loved it. For a few months I was filling in at Victor Harbor Hospital where I had begun my nursing in 1972. I was totally shocked when the nurses told me the 'old nurses quarters' was demolished and now a car park for the new extended hospital. I took many photos back in 2014 specifically for this book. Just for the memories of patients I nursed.

Mum was slowly deteriorating, but was still ambulant around the nursing home. She had made some friends too, that was mum all over, always making friends. However, there were some signs to me that these were going to be her last months and wanted them to be her best. Mum and I used to have some deep conversations mostly about my childhood and my marriages. I never realized how much we had in common. She also expressed that she appreciated me coming back to SA to help take care of her. Mum knew what I had given up to leave my highest paying job and my studies. Life didn't seem all about me that day, this was my mother who went through life the best way she could, against the odds. Her life was almost over and she knew it. No second chances, she had done her best. She told me she loved me and it had taken so long to hear that. We hugged we laughed we cried. My special moment with my mother. We were too much alike but wouldn't admit it till now. It did not matter what made us upset with each other, we were part of a bond that DNA couldn't lie about. I thought of my own daughter. She cannot break our DNA bond, no matter how she tries. My daughter and her husband at the time along with her children, my grandchildren, visited mum in October 2012. We had canvas prints of the kids and a maternal shot of my mum, myself, my daughter and my granddaughter on 6th October the day they returned to Qld.

On the 10th October 2012 my mum passed away. Am sure she was just waiting for Melanie. They were close. My sister was devastated; she was so close to mum. I felt sad for her as she had done so much for mum and now she was on her own. Dad and Mum are both in heaven now. No grandparents, very strange feeling, like an orphan. We only had our siblings now. Our own children and grandchildren. The circle of life. It was a very sad day and the whole family came together. Looking back at different family photos, of gatherings I could see the ones who were missing in the next gathering. It is more of a reminder that the pictures are reflective of our lives going past too fast. Not long after my mum passed away, I was diagnosed with cancer. Precancerous cells were detected which began a series of tests and procedures. After 12 months of abnormal results and getting very paranoid about the outcome the oncologist did a series of medical procedures requiring day surgery. Nothing changed. My friend Diana kept me going by watching over me, determined to not let this cancer turn into something terrible. I was working full-time and was waiting for a solution to arrange sick leave. Another year went past, still have cancer cells. My GP at the time tried to investigate exactly what was happening.

Being an absolute wreck and nurses always make the worst patients, we know too much. I tried to keep myself busy with work and the secretarial role with NHW and SDRA. I held meetings, generated all information to the Chairperson, Treasurer, SAPOL, and collected data on local crime and NHW. It was also part of my role to prepare a selection of guest speakers to the monthly meetings, such as the local Mayor, Construction Companies on local main works. Health ministers at the time and several other politicians. As it was one per month it filled up my time between nursing, caring for my mum, and NHW. The local construction developers had extended my area of houses and families to visit. I received many complaints as the secretary from residents about different issues ranging from the grass too high on the verge and on a nearby bus stop. So one Saturday the Mayor, the Chairperson, Treasurer, and myself took a ride in a car and checked every verge, and any other issues round the neighborhood. I put together a letter to the council regards to their scheduled maintenance planning. Basically an improved an updated outcome was presented to me prior to the next meeting. I must have had some old 'mover and shaker 'left in me.

I had a wonderful working relationship with the police, the residents of the townships and always on top of the taking of the minutes. A new housing development started and I went door to door giving away new tote bags with information on Local Neighborhood Watch and SDRA meetings. I called it 'The

Welcome Pack'. The tote also had freebies and items for kids, leftover toys etc. from the Royal Adelaide Show. There was so much response it was amazing. Sometimes I would hold the Executive meetings at my house. At one point we organized drinking bowls and taps along the foreshore for dogs to be able to drink fresh water when they went walking with their owners. So many things we did for the community. I was even invited officially to Parliament House by the Health Minister. My mum was alive then and she was very proud indeed. She herself had been formally invited to Parliament House by a former politician.

I had kept up appointments at the new Cancer Centre at Flinders Hospital, and I was getting a bit overwhelmed regarding all these procedures and still finding cancer cells. The decision was made to do a complete hysterectomy. Well I was scared, relied a lot on my close friends and family, I would see ads on TV regarding 'cancer nurses' give them a call anytime. After about 3 weeks I was getting concerned that the longer they left this cancer inside me, the less chance I had of surviving. I was overwhelmed and wish my mum was here to hug me, even dad. One day at work I was having staff knocking at my door constantly, mainly non urgent problems. Like they weren't dying of cancer! Diana worked in the office next to me at the time. I went in, locked the door and had a good cry. Feeling relieved and supported, she suggested I call the cancer hotline just to ease my mind. I did. It was amazing, the understanding and support I received was so helpful. They asked for my Oncologist name and my diagnosis. I told them everything. On duty the next day, I received a call from the Flinders Hospital admissions advising me my surgery for the hysterectomy would be on 29th May! OMG that was only 3 days away!

So now I knew when and what and finally, hopefully I will be cancer free. My sister came with me to the admissions. I went in, had the surgery, and survived. Home in 4 days. Friends and family visited me at home, Diana came after work and stayed till late, bringing her sky with beer and cigarettes. She was set for the day. It took a while to get used to the pain when walking about as the bedroom was at the front of the house and the kitchen and living areas way down the other end. Shopping online became a hit. During the recovery period I decided to take my sister and my nephew on holiday to Cairns for 5 days. It was the best thing to get me back on track. Margaret had a great birthday too, my eldest son and his daughter visited as they were in the area due to his wife being in her friend's wedding the same weekend! We took so many photos that the resort was spectacular.

Things were getting back to normal, I went back to work in the duty manager role in Mental Health, kept the Secretarial position with SDRA and NHW with SAPOL. It wasn't easy but I got through it all. Mum used to say 'Us women were strong and could survive anything' perhaps she was right, but there were times I wasn't so sure about that. I was sitting at my desk at home, typing up minutes for the next NHW meeting when the chair that I was obviously sitting on fell backwards and flipped. I landed right on my coccyx. The pain was immediate, sharp, splitting and I think I passed out for a few moments as my cat, Maddie was licking my face and meowing. I crawled to my bedroom to grabbed some spare panadeine forte tabs, which didn't help so carefully drove to local ED. The Nurse Practitioner took me in straight away organized an X ray and gave me an Endone. After the X ray was done and checked by the doctor, I was experiencing just a dull ache as the Endone had kicked in. Yes, they confirmed I had fractured my coccyx, totally but there wasn't any surgery to fix it. Natural healing, rest and pain relief. So beggar that was it. The Nurse Practitioner gave me the discharge letter for the GP and I was to follow up with him. Anything serious come back to ED or call 000.

Lying on my bed at home I was waiting till I took the next panadeine forte, before calling the surgery to make an appointment, no rush I thought. The receptionist put me down straight away for urgent appointment. I made an effort to drive with my buttocks off the seat, to drive the short distant to the surgery. My GP was marvelous, he gave me a medicate certificate for Centrelink for 3 months. Well that was that! I actually still attended the SDRA meeting with apologies for me not being quite with it as I felt off my face on pain killers. The local police laughed and said they would drive me home. I declined. I had to go to Centrelink and that was just the worst experience. The last shift I did would actually pay my rent, but I had a plethora of medications and did not have the money. At Centrelink I asked nicely to speak to a Social Worker, some red haired lady served me, not a social worker, and she was not helpful at all despite my GP had completed and signed the form. Apparently I wasn't entitled to anything as l was classed as 'working' and had to use other funds. What the hell were 'other funds'? For four weeks! I burst out crying, being more angry and frustrated plus I could 'take a seat 'as I couldn't sit, I had a cracked arse!

The security guy was walking towards my direction. Honestly I could have taken him out I was so angry. I was standing and ready to punch him if he had grabbed my arm. Suddenly another lady, a real social worker, came over a quietly spoke to me. We had a ten-minute conversation and then she looked over my form and then my file on her computer.

"Let me sort this out, go home and rest. A man named Darrin will call you in a couple of hours". She promised me that I would get my Health Concession Card for my medications. I drove home again, set pillows up at end of my bed, laid on my stomach to watch TV while Maddie laid next to me. I had nodded off to sleep through sheer mental exhaustion and my phone ringing woke me up. It was the guy from Centrelink. Great news! He approved my Health Care Concession card and I can collect it at the front desk, no need to line up. He also granted me $161.00 being over 60 years plus in a weeks' time I would receive a full fortnightly payment! I was so grateful to him. I only had to present my lease and I would get rent assistance on top of that. Immediately I drove a bit faster than usual back to the Centrelink office, didn't care about the pain. I collected my medication on the way home and just rested with Maddie on the bed for the rest of the afternoon. Why do I need to fight for everything that I am entitled to from the Government?

As I progressed for the next few months with varying levels of pain, I took time off from attending general meetings at SDRA and NHW, but worked from home to deal with correspondence in and out. Contacted councils, SAPOL etc. by phone and emails. My GP saw me regularly and signed various documents for income insurance support. It paid the rent and paid the bills. Eventually it all ran out and the reality set in that I would need to go back to work soon. Unfortunately, the GP had not cleared me fit enough to return to work. He had also put me on anti-depressants. I needed to find other accommodation. This was not easy when you are single, over 60 and have a cat. I had no choice to settle on a retirement unit, one bedroom and small courtyard. In actual fact it was quite nice, new and close to shopping center in short walking distance. They included meals and charged like over $200 per fortnight and the meals were not that great. Fatty and so bad for my diabetes. It was on medical reasons that I was able to stop paying $200 and buy my own food, for less than $ 100 per fortnight. I had a brand new BBQ in my courtyard and cooked up lots of healthy meals.

It was sad to have to sell my Grand Cherokee Jeep. Nowhere to park it, only one car per unit. I had to sell my new caged trailer. At the time my dear friend Diana had 2 dogs so it wasn't possible to keep my cat there, but that was ok. I settled into the retirement village and I had already downsized quite a bit. From a 3-bedroom home with 2 living areas, 2 bathrooms and huge yard to a one bedroom unit with bath and laundry and small courtyard. Hey this is my life now. Well for now anyway. I did feel a bit uncomfortable with close neighbors, being elderly or disabled and asking for help as they found out I was a nurse. The constant ambulances going in and out at all hours was off putting. I felt too young to be living there while neighbors were dying. New ones moved in, old ones died out. My neighbor tried to commit suicide and giving her two little Jack Russell dogs poison. I tried to help and broke into her unit, through a sliding door and called an ambulance. She survived, the dogs didn't. Living amongst the aged was not as fun and I knew I wasn't going to stay more than a year. The managers did nothing to help, apparently not their responsibility.

Most residents ate their meals in the dining room. Sort of like a meeting place with a library, computer and amenities such as toilet and a laundry, which I didn't know about at first, had my own washing machine. When it was lunch time you queued up at the server, I really didn't mind as it was just like being in the nurses quarters where we all lined up in the dining room. Luckily here were no Matrons to stand up for, however this was similar to a dining room in an aged care facility and I was not ready to be in that category yet.! Some were choking, spilling drinks or their food. It was quite off putting for me, as a nurse it seemed like I was supposed to assist feed. When I was working the kitchen staff would keep my meals in the fridge with my unit number on it. Worked out fine for a while until someone stole my meal, and it was my favourite one, silverside cauliflower white sauce with vegies and Pavlova for dessert! Every diabetic loves a treat and Pavlova was my weakness.

I met lots of residents in the dining room. Some were nice, most were cranky old men. Of course there were the old guys on the 'prowl' as it were. No way! I met Wayne who was another Essendon supporter and we got along well. The other two guys at his table were a bit jealous and were acting like school boys. Not long after that Wayne stopped going to the dining room. I thought I had offended him somehow. The fact was he found a loophole regards to not being required to pay for the food. Apparently you could opt out and buy your own food but you could not cook in your unit. We started having BBQs at my place. Maddie soon got used to him. Sometimes I would stay over for work at Murray Bridge at the nurse's quarters, $10 bucks a night. That was a sweet deal as it took me 90 minutes each way to get to work. As I was still doing Nursing

Agency work, even though I loved my job as Duty Manager at the Community Mental Health Team and getting very well paid for it. However, I had this desire since I was 14 years of age to go to Paris. Loving everything French, the language, the fashions, the food, I needed a fulltime job where I would get annual leave paid and have a steady job to come back to after my trip. I had applied for a passport, received it while I was recuperating from my Hysterectomy surgery a couple of years prior. I asked my daughter and granddaughter if they would like to go for my 60th birthday. My granddaughter loved everything French also, sadly my daughter declined. I was willing to pay for all of us, flights and accommodation. But still got a no.

Thinking I should brush up on my French from St. Mary's College I got a French to English dictionary. I also had been given a book about Paris from a guy I used to date, at the time we were right into the 'Hunger Games' and he used to call me 'Miss Hotness'. Always made me laugh. Unfortunately, as much as I enjoyed his company and all the places we would visit, we ended the relationship. We had dated many years prior like 18 years earlier and I hoped we would pick up where we left it. Alas it was wonderful while it lasted I wanted more than he was willing to give. Originally when we were dating in 1998, I was struggling to get over my ex-husband, yes the one I haven't talked about … yet, and with our recent catch up in 2014, this time he was struggling to get over an ex-girlfriend. Karma bit me hard. Well guess it wasn't to be. But it was great while it lasted. We ended it somewhat mutually.

Chapter 9:
You Can't Make This Shit Up.

This chapter is dedicated to my fabulous friend, Darling Diana. Over the years my friend Diana and I have been through some crazy times, funny times, and stuff you just wouldn't believe. But it did happen and still happens and we still laugh about it rather than cry or get angry. We never got angry with each other in almost 30 years of friendship. The fabulous Diana has a way about her that seems to glide through life and has a calming effect on those around her inner circle. That's the magic of her. She has been and always will be my friend, confidant, best coworker, and absolutely the most outrageous and caring person I know. Diana has a caring nature with some ruthless daredevil traits. She'll tell you honestly no bullshit or tiptoeing around, if you want her opinion, and sometimes even when you don't she'll give you the truth straight up. Diana is not an arrogant or persistent character but just the right amount of awesome.

We met in 1996, I had been going through a depressed state after the sudden ending of my last and final marriage. Everything was going wrong and I just couldn't get my shit together as much as I tried. My parents were living in South Australia still and were very supportive and my dad was amazing and told me to move down to the beachy side of South Adelaide near them. Best choice I ever made at that time for both myself and my youngest son, to recover mentally, emotionally, and financially from my divorce, which I did not want …. ever! So Michael and I moved to the beach at Silver Sands and began our recovery. I became stronger and managed to get a job as an Enrolled Nurse at Christies Beach and life began again for us. My youngest sister lived not far from us at Lading Beach and it was so good to be near family again. She had her own lifestyle and friends and actually, we didn't have that much in common, but we were sisters, we were family and that counts for everything.

From the first day at work, Diana was the one who took me under her wing and introduced me to the staff, and made me feel part of the team. Most of the girls I met that week are still friends with me today. Diana has always been the glue that held us all together and I am sure they would agree. Diana had this knack of maneuvering things like getting days off for New Year's Eve parties by inviting the boss, and then requesting the next day off as if it was an afterthought. She always got the day off! That's her brilliance and everybody loved her. I loved her. We were all watching the funeral of Lady Diana at work, we were all saddened by this epic event. All the residents and staff wept as we watched it on TV in the dining room. It felt like we were actually there in London. It was unbelievable and soul crushing to see those two young boys walking behind their mother's coffin. What a procession indeed. Recently whilst at Diana's house she introduced me to the Netflix series 'The Crown'. I was so into it and every night I would watch a few episodes with her to catch up before the new series began. Absolutely enjoyed it and learnt a lot. Just prior to that, I had read Prince Harry's book Spare.

In the late 90s every Friday or Saturday night was party night get together at 'The Lodge'. The name Diana gave her house on the Esplanade opposite the beach, with fabulous views of the ocean. As I worked afternoon shifts I could only go to the Lodge after work to join in. All the gang were drinking, laughing and just generally having a good time. I used to stay late at to this day don't know how I did it, but I would leave her place about 3am and drive home which took about 30 minutes. I always made it home safely, amazingly! Every time this Matchbox Twenty song would come on the radio, 3am I still think of those evening at Diana's Lodge. We laughed about it even in 2024. I recall one time Diana had been out somewhere and ended up at a bus stop early in the morning. She didn't know how she got there and had misplaced her work shirt. It was hilarious at the time. Fortunately, she found one and made it to work. It had been one of those blurry moments.

One night my son and I stayed over at Diana's with the plan to get up early and drive my son to the Franklin St. bus station to catch the Coach to Melbourne to visit his father. Well the night was full of laughter, friends and alcohol. Even when everyone else left, Diana and I stayed up and chatted till 3am. Long story short, we all slept in. OMG it was like panic on steroids everyone running around like maniacs, even Michael who was panicking about missing his Coach. I personally hated being late for anything, so this caused a new sensation. Not sure what happen with my car, but it wouldn't start, so we had to take Diana's station wagon and after we called the bus terminal, no mobile phones then, explained our dilemma. Next stop was Crafters. Off we went like crazy cats being scolded! We made it, everyone could now breathe. Phew just in time for the coach, don't know how I would explain to his father. This was our first 'You couldn't make up this shit 'events. One of many to come over the years.

There were a few incidents at work that became fond memories, we all had our roles to play but we always did it as a team. If someone was behind in their schedule to do an unfortunate episode of explosive motions just after a shower and was close to their meal break, no worries mate, a couple of staff would help out with undressing, quick showering down then one nurse would dry and dress the resident. No bitchiness, no complaints we would just get in and get the job done! Everyone knew how to help each other, although there were Registered nurses, Enrolled nurses and personal careers, we were a team in the 90's.Everyone was a personal career, everyone was a nurse. We were the best team and we loved working together. Music from a distant radio would be audible throughout the wards and we sung along, we did our jobs. I recall working with Nikki who was an awesome nurse and we did a few afternoons together. We were bathing this lady in the blue bath which was a medical hospital long bath with wheels and hydraulics that went higher or lower and sides down and up to ensure the resident couldn't roll out. Nikki and I would roll her onto this soft rubbery bath and wheel her to the bathroom. We would sing

"Slide with me, slide with me" and dance to the music to the music of a song playing in the background. We did our job well.

These were good memories of not just nursing but of comradeship. It was a special group of women whose friendship stayed forever, even when they went interstate, married, had children or just travelling around the globe. I had always been nursing and glad I did as it was something I could go back to even after relationship breakups, the friends were always there. When I was married to Shane my baby was only 6 weeks old when I had to return to work part-time. As I have mentioned before it was very hard for me leaving this precious baby behind, despite being cared for by relatives. My sister in law was very good with Bradley – Shane and will always be grateful for her assistance at that time. The early mornings, freezing weather, catching public transport, and worst of all missing my son. Most of the shifts were where nobody wanted to work, or hard to get to by public transport. The walks from the bus stops or rail stations in the early dark mornings were scary, sometimes pelting down with rain with cold winds. The back streets of western Sydney were not really safe on your own. These days are worse and women have been murdered in those areas. No mobile phones, couldn't afford taxi cabs, and definitely no Ubers. One slight good advantage was that if I got a shift in a major hospital the buses actually stopped there. It came to a point where Shane and I decided I would just work weekends, whereas the advantage was that Shane would be there for Bradley – Shane and eliminate childcare costs and I could drive the car to work and be safer.

It seemed like a win-win situation. I had quality time during the week with my baby who was evolving into a cute chubby toddler. We had planned our wedding on Australia Day weekend, 1977. I had the weekend off, it was a quiet wedding as noted before just family and friends … mainly his mates, I don't recall having any friends at my wedding. Such a shame. Things unfortunately changed a bit after that, Shane became more distant, aloof and only paid attention to the now talking toddler that followed his daddy everywhere, and of course Uncle Derek, the Godfather. Glenn became more attentive to me, such a good friend especially when I had a car accident coming home from work one Sunday. Of course all the guys were at our place with Shane. Some jerk had hit me from behind at the traffic lights. I guess he didn't notice it was a red light or the fact I had already stopped! He jumped out of his car at the same time I did but I was doing all the yelling.

He looked at the mess of both vehicles checking the damage. My Cortina had the worst damage.

"Oh shit. I am so sorry, I didn't realize you were a girl! He looked really upset and then added, "My wife is going to kill me, it's the third one this month!"

I looked at him still stunned by the 'girl' comment and really concerned about the admission of a third accident. No mobile phones. To make things worse I was on my 'P' plates... just.

"Well don't worry about your wife, as my husband is going to kill you first. You will need to follow me home to Cabramatta so we can let my husband see it". He tried to tell me we couldn't report it to the police as I was only on 'P' plates and would go straight to jail. Well I yelled back at him and informed him that I didn't care as I didn't cause the accident! I couldn't believe it this man actually followed me from Ashfield to Cabramatta with my car only able to do about 20 kiss / hour. Maybe back then in 1977 it may have been miles per hour. Anyway it was a very slow drive home.

I really had a bad day at work. During my shift I was asked to give this patient her 'Depot' injection for her Schizophrenia condition, which I had never done so far in my career. On entering the room a well-dressed lady was sitting in a chair, she stated she was visiting and she'd gone out somewhere. I went back twice. The RN came with me and said that was the patient and to just give it to her. She watched as I injected her in the arm. I definitely wasn't sure if I really wanted to be injecting people with mental health disorders. It just wasn't my preferred area of nursing. Thinking about that day decades later made me smile as in later years I actually ran the Depot Clinic for Mental Health. After the car accident, I had a throbbing headache by the time I got home. Shane and Derek were checking out the car, examining all the damage, and talking to the guy who hit me. Not one person asked if I was ok. Finally, Glenn enquired if I got hurt. When I told him my neck hurt a lot and I had a massive headache, he followed me upstairs to the apartment and got me a couple of Panadol and a glass of water. I thanked him. He suggested I see a GP in case I had to claim damages with the insurance.

Apparently, the Cortina was a write-off, a cut and shut as Derek called it as he was the apprentice mechanic and everyone listened to his opinions. It became a little more complicated as the guy's wife had turned up and there was a question as to the insurance being paid late. One of our neighbors' worked for his insurance company so the next two days were sorting out this dilemma. Long story short the insurance claim was paid and we bought a Valiant Charger. Good car, like a tank. We drove it to Adelaide for a holiday! Never went back to that ward in Ashfield again. The GP checked me out, did bloods and filled out forms in case it was a worker's compensation claim later on. Gp mentioned 'whip lash' so I went back a couple days later. Unfortunately he could prescribe me only Panadol for the neck pain as I was pregnant! OMG I was so surprised and elated. I hoped it was a girl. I waited till I had the first opportunity to tell Shane, when his mates weren't hanging around as they normal did. I was expecting a hug, a kiss at least some type of enthusiasm on his part. Sadly, for me he wasn't impressed, and we had an argument over it. 'Wasn't I still on the pill?', 'How could this happen'? 'One child is enough!' it just went on and on. I just broke down and cried. We were married, why couldn't I have this baby, I was already 3 months pregnant. I wanted a daughter, blonde hair with blue eyes. I sat in the bathroom for almost an hour crying. No matter what I was going to have this baby.

I could understand his issue with me having stop working for a while but really it should not have been a huge issue. He was definitely a loving father, patient, giving and the best father to Bradley – Shane. You just couldn't separate them, two peas in a pod. When the time came to let family and friends know about the pregnancy, everyone was so happy for us. Almost. We were at a BBQ at Glenn's parents' house where he cornered me behind the fridge door and whispered to me,

"I was willing to look after you and Bradley, but no way could I take care of my mate's child, that would be wrong and he's my best mate. I am so sorry." He really did look sad his honesty was totally understandable, having said that did not have any intentions of leaving Shane with our baby on the way. He deserved better than that. Still praying for a girl, but if it was a boy, I hoped it was as placid as Bradley was as a baby and a toddler. He would play for hours with his match box cars and Lego. The days were wonderful and motherhood was as it should be. This pregnancy should go smoothly with no major issues.

As the family was expanding to four we had to move house. We did, we liked the house even though the colors were a bit out there, blue on outside with some walls inside were yellow and some were green. It may have had a Greek theme around the neighborhood. The third bedroom received a good lick of pink paint, the wardrobe was pink and white and same for the cot. Shane was hoping for a boy only so we didn't need to buy new clothes. Had crossed my fingers for a girl, or I had just wasted a lot of paint. During the last trimester we had a few issues which were mainly caused by other people. Two young ladies, and I use that term loosely, knocked on my door looking for Shane and Derek and literally got shoved out the way as they proceeded down to the kitchen! How did they know where the kitchen was? Despite being 8 months pregnant I was not impressed. My first thought was 'bitches'! Well there was a lot of shouting, pushing and agree bargy so to speak, mainly on my part. Hormones we'll say for now. Shane left with Derek. We argued on his return. We got physically aggressive, I recall throwing a mug in his direction. I fell asleep on the couch. Two days later I had an obstetrician appointment and when the specialist noticed the bruising over most of my belly he asked to see my husband. I was terrified, just like in my first marriage. Any physical type of threat or injury just terrified me, it was soul-destroying, I knew he would not let any harm come to his boy. At this point I just wanted to have this baby and get on with my life.

My mum had flown to America and Canada to visit her cousin Lois and her daughters, who lived in California. My baby was due while she was away. Christmas wasn't far away and this baby was due 24th December 1977. Christmas came and went. No baby, People kept asking me, "Have you not had that baby yet!" I was sick of hearing it! I was watching my favourite soap show, and the actress who was my favourite character was named Lauralie and her on screen boyfriend was Brad (where I came up with the name for Bradley) I seriously wanted to call this baby, if a girl, Lauralie and wanting to give her the family middle name of Caroline, but saying it out loud was too much LaLalayt.Bradley couldn't say it. I think Shane had a hankering for Faye after his mum. We had no ideas on a boy's name. Did I mention I really wanted a girl? It was a very hot summer in 1977, we didn't have air conditioning and I was heavy as a few days overdue. Thinking back on when Bradley was overdue and no one believed me until he was born. The only thing I recalled is the Midwife, Melanie, saying after delivering my first baby in 15 minutes,

"If you have another baby you better come in early as second babies are normally quicker".

Being so hot and uncomfortable, exhausted and fed up with Shane not helping (not sure what the poor bugger was supposed to do)I decided to take myself off to the hospital. Was a great idea I thought, the hospital had air conditioning. Didn't really think it quite through, I couldn't fit behind the steering wheel to even drive to hospital. Of course I couldn't reach the pedals either. Shane came out in a huff to see what I was doing. He laughed when he saw I couldn't fit in the car to drive. I just sat there and cried and saying

"I am having this baby tonight!".

Like the trooper he was he just went inside to get my hospital bag and Bradley – Shane plus his overnight 'nana' bag. Shane put him in the back seat and whispered, "You're lucky son you are going to nana's house and mummy's going to hospital." Grandpa was excited waiting for his little mate to come and stay. Arriving at Fairfield Hospital we went straight to maternity unit. They were busy and I had to say I was having contractions otherwise they would have sent me home. Shane could see the desperation on my face, we did get a midwife to check me out. Only 3cm and no contractions, it was clear I was not in labor. The coolness in the holding ward was much appreciated. My specialist was about to leave and go on holidays for Christmas break, it was now the evening of the 26th December. I heard him say to the midwife that I wasn't in labor and my waters were still intact. They made a decision to book me in for an induction 8am Tuesday. I thought yay!

Tomorrow I should have my baby. Well it was Tuesday 27th my waters were broken by the obstetrician with a long set of forceps and no warning, it was not my finest hour. Nothing happened all day, all night. Shane stayed for hours, then left for hours, then came back until a nurse told him nothing was going to happen and he could go home. So he did he looked so tired and almost felt sorry for him until contractions came intermittently. I was placed into a holding bay, there were 3 other mothers to be in beds. Curtains separating us. It was only about 8 pm but the lights were out and we could only see a little bit of light from the nurse's station. When the night shift nurse came on she said to one of the ladies,

"Now I can't give you anything unless you ask me for it, totally up to you."

"Yes please I would like the injection." I heard a woman say. The nurse came back closed the curtain and gave her an injection. Within the hour, no kidding she was ringing the bell and taken to the labor ward. The sound of a baby crying was heard down the hall. Wow how quick was that, this happened again and within an hour her baby was born. I couldn't sleep with wondering what was in this injection. By the time the third and last woman had the magic injection, it was daylight and day staff were coming on.

After waiting for my obstetrician to come it was ten o'clock. The baby was in a weird position and hoped it wasn't a breech birth. Contractions were happening but not fast enough. There were lots of decisions made and I wasn't included in the discussion. Shane came in and stayed by my side. The nurses were saying not long now, it was now after dinner, oh no I couldn't eat … just in case. Well by the time 10.30pm came around and the night nurse was cruising around, I told Shane about her and her magic injections. My body was feeling pushed and the specialists came back in about 11pm. Me by this stage was begging for a Caesarean no anesthetic required as it couldn't be any more painful.

The Midwife starts getting gowned up and things were happening. No the midwife couldn't tell me the sex of the baby. Shane was asked "What are you hoping for". He looked at me, then the doctor.

"For my sake it better be a girl!" he said holding my hand. I smiled at him and thought, your poor bugger I must have given you hell. Strong contractions started. Yes, am having this baby NOW.

Strong, long and took hours of pain, strain, push and rest. The problem was the baby had its hands across my pelvis and wouldn't be born, just little hands in the way. Another intervention by the team. I wanted to sleep, I needed to sleep. At 1240am on the 29th December I had my baby girl. Shane and I were shocked at how dark her hair was and lots of it. We both thought, oh it must have been those Chinese meals I craved for. She was here at last. That's it no more for me, I'm done. We held her and just smiled at her. She was absolutely beautiful; Faye would be pleased to see her latest granddaughter. They took her to wash and do her checks. They washed me and took me to my room. I was in the bathroom and a nurse came in with a needle, she just pulled up my nighty exposing my thigh, oh yes she must be positive, she was AB+ and I was O-, so got the anti D shot like my first bubs. Getting settled into my bed, not that hospital beds are comfortable, but I had a few hectic days without sleep. Was just nodding off when at 2.40am some cheery bloody voice says,

"Let's try a little breast feeding ?" I do remember unwrapping her pink blanket and counting her fingers and toes with Shane, proud as punch with his daughter. I then rewrapped her and buzzed for the nurse. I explain to the nurse I had no sleep for days, please give her a bottle in the nursery just for the night. She looked a bit shocked but took her to the nursery. I hardly remember Shane kissing me goodbye as he left, I had fallen into a deep sleep. I was content and looked forward to little Bradley seeing his baby sister.

Chapter 10:
7 Days in Paris – Bonjour !

My heart was set on Paris. I decided to leave the Retirement place as I felt way too young to be living there, so I looked for another local place that I could afford and save for my first ever overseas adventure. Wayne noticed a 'to rent' sign next door in a block of 8 units which were owned by a private landlord. I said for him to get the number and I would check with him tomorrow. We chatted about the unit, private landlord sounded good, 2 bedrooms and a bigger courtyard, all sounded good. As I was planning to go to Paris and Wayne was going to be watching Maddie for me, we thought why not share the unit. So we did just that. Maddie settled in well and was already Wayne's shadow. The advantages would be more room, a kitchen to cook in, financially share the rent and expenses and Maddie would know the neighborhood still. In the meantime, my youngest granddaughter was about to be born. I booked my flights and accommodation for Paris and London, and then drove to Traralgon for the birth of precious Caroline. While we were about to drive back to Adelaide, we received the good news that we were approved for the new unit. I think adrenaline kept us pumped for the long drive home.

Physically moving furniture, personal items from both our units was exhausting, I was working full time, plus getting excited about my trip to Paris, I think that was the only thing keeping me going. I flew to Paris via China on 4th June 2017. The most memorable holiday of my life! I guess I was nervous going on my own, at 61 years of age. I hoped to visit my aunt Mavis in Germany. All I had was her phone number. I had told my cousin Damien that I was going to Europe and would love to catch up. We actually had plans but nothing happened, no answer on phone either. My sister was in contact with him and his brothers, but no reply for me. I thought that was strange actually and disappointing.

From the time I was in the International Airport in Adelaide, to go to China I was very relaxed. My brain wandered to my friend Diana, who requested a sexy black French nightie. Ha-ha, got we're all getting old and that was all she wanted as a souvenir. My thoughts were interrupted by my name being called over the PA. I almost wet myself. So nervously walked over to the China Southern counter where the aircrew lady asked for my ticket and passport. Well I was very scared then, expecting security to grab me. My friends Lisa, Phil and Wayne would be on their way home by then. OMG can I ring my sister or Diana for help. I handed the lady my documents, hands shaking the whole time. With a pleasant surprise she handed me an upgraded ticket to Premium as it was spare and I was travelling alone! She also handed me a tote bag with lots of goodies inside, a blanket and a pillow as well! Once on board and settled into my seat the Air Hostess delivered some coffee with an amazing aroma. There was plenty of leg room and only 2 seats, I had the window seat and no seats behind me, so I could recline to almost sleeping position. So far I was enjoying this fancy trip, also checking out the TV screen in front of me with so many channels to choice from and included the head phones.

Again the crew came around with some delicious 3 course meal, being lunch I presume, we only departed at 10am. After devouring the different but flavorsome meal I watched two movies, did two walks up and down the plane, a snooze and a hot white novelette to freshen up. Wow next came another meal. Dinner? Again a full three course meal and coffee. China Southern had the best take offs and landings. Looking out my window I could see the wing. So large spread out for what seemed a kilometer. Awesome trip, and the young man sitting next to me, Matthew, he had an upgrade to, he was going to India via China. He was married and going to see a sick relative in India. He was Australian. He slept a lot during the flight, with his earphones in his ears. Quiet lad, I felt bad when I had to wake him to let me out to go to the bathroom. He was very accommodating.

Next thing I knew we had landed at Guangzhou Airport, China. Very daunting trying to get through customs. Queuing up to show your passports with guards at every checkpoint, armed guards who did not smile but looked straight through you. The customs men were worse, and he looked at my passport then at my face three times. Finally, he let me pass. What a relief. It was so busy, it was night and there were so many people waiting to go to their own destinations. Security guards wandered through looking at people, long rifles pointed at the ready. This was not a custom in Australia that I was used to at all. Apart from locating the toilets, it was a learning curve, look at the doors, note to self. First one had a grate over a square hole in the floor. No idea what the hell to make of that, do I squat? No way I am not that desperate. I did see a door with a drawing of a toilet on it, could this be a real toilet inside.? Yay so much relief to see some normal, so obviously spent a penny as mum would say. I had already been to the money exchange to get 100 yen. Had no idea the exchange rate until I went to get a coffee. Couldn't believe there was a McDonald's right there in the airport! So there was a language barrier with the young server and myself, not understanding 'Coffee please'. Lucky the menu had pictures! I handed her my 100-yen note, counting my change it was only 1.83 yen that seemed cheap to me. I went checking out souvenirs for my latest granddaughter, like a Panda bear.

I finally located a seat outside the gate 103 for Air France to take me to Paris. I was getting sleepy at this stage this must be jet lag that travelers talk about. The time of departure to Paris was 2305hrs to arrive in CDG Airport at 0555hrs. Thinking of how nice would it be to see the sunrise in Paris! I already had an amazing memory of going over the equator. Truly an experience indeed. Drinking my McCabe coffee and sitting at the Gate 103 I wondered what gifts I would get in London and Paris for my grandchildren back in Australia. This being the most exciting trip of my life. I thought about my dad and how we used to speak in French at home. Great memories, now I wished he was with me, but guess his spirit would be there. I wondered how Wayne and Maddie were going, would they be missing me or perhaps not… At that time, I thought of him being my rock in life. I even thought we would be old together, no nursing homes for us. Maybe we could do some travels, perhaps to Canada where his father was born. We will see, no promises.

Well just sitting waiting for the gate to open for boarding, OMG still 45 minutes to go, could I stay awake? Looking at my ticket I think I get another meal on this flight, it says so on my ticket. If I do I will eat, sleep, watch a movie and sleep again till I get to Paris. That was the plan anyway. Tried to check my mobile, no internet, there was a message from Optus about 'roaming charges'. Turned it off. No point in having it on as no one will be calling or texting me. Once I get to Paris I can buy an international pre-paid card and call my sister and Wayne. Am feeling a bit safer in China, many people coming and going, not many Aussies but mostly Chinese, Africans and quite a few Indians. The time says 2055 on the Flight Gate clock, says 2230hrs on my watch. One hour till boarding, I may be asleep by then but aware of my luggage and personal items, not trusting any travelers around me. At last, on the plane to Paris, very tired. The Air France crew not as friendly as the China Southern crew, but with a smile now and then and a 'bonjour' helped along the way. The crew was bringing a huge cane basket tray with more food. French menu of course, chocolate Croissants with French-brewed coffee. The main meal had some unusual types of vegetables but the dessert was absolutely delicious. After watching a couple of movies I nodded off, could hardly keep my eyes open at all. Stretching out after my nanny nap I checked the air flight screen. Only 5 hours till we arrive in Paris. Two hours prior to landing we were given another full-course meal. Guess it was dinner who knew? It was food and of course the famous Croissants, hot and fresh. I noticed the Japanese passengers were constantly up and down, some going to the bathroom and others were just standing in the aisle getting in the way of the crew who were trying to serve other passengers. No sorry or anything, just plain rude actually!

I snuggled back into my seat and watched another movie. Soon enough the sunrise could have been seen and we were making our descent into CDG Airport Paris, France. I was amazed but disappointed I couldn't see the Eiffel Tower as I had expected for the last 45 minutes! Touchdown at 0555hrs, looking like any other airport at first. Once disembarked off the plane and walking across a tarmac, we were all met by a train that pulls up to take passengers to the airport. Lots of noisy French announcements can be heard, security showing people where to go, ok so I get on this train, hang onto hand rails keep an eye on your luggage, passports and body parts. Very cramped and only takes a few minutes as it travels so fast to customs section of the airport. Here is the scary part. The passengers were met by men with rifles pointed at you gesturing to move quickly and guards were checking your passports and tickets. I saw an opening and thought it was the exit, four armed officers moved swiftly towards me and a lady officer stopped me by grabbing my passport. I was so upset, couldn't think of any French words, but I demanded my passport back! Apparently I was going out the wrong exit, so the armed guards escorted me to the correct exit. For sure that would be on TV Border Control, so I went through the checkout point and the lady in uniform returned my passport. No smiles, just waded through the several gates. All good and passed through to the taxi and transfers signs were. Phew glad that was over, welcome to Paris!

Once I was actually outside the enormous airport I checked the number of the transfer company. I went inside to ask at the transfer counter, she showed me the number on my itinerary, I had to call them myself. I was informed to wait at Gate 16. Unfortunately, I could not find any Gate 16. Everything was numbered like 2D 6A etc. A chubby chap got out of his taxi like vehicle and headed straight for me.

"Madam you go to Paris with transfer? he spoke pretty good English for a Frenchman. I showed him my documents with my pre-paid transfer and accommodation information. He smiled and indicated towards his taxi, placing my suitcase in the boot. I was the only passenger. So far so good. During our drive we went through the tunnel that Lady Diana had her accident and subsequently died. I felt a little sad and would have to tell my friend Diana of this adventure. The time seemed so slow getting to my Motel, Pavilion Carcelle's Marceau, saw the street sign and got very excited. There it was, Rue De Saussure Paris! Wow I was in Paris! The chubby driver smiled and then said the fare was 63 euros, this shocked me as I had paid for this transfer! I questioned him about this. He said "Not Uber transfer, not me, it is 63 euros thank you Madam" I thought ok, lesson no.1. I had to pay and really pissed off about the whole thing.

The foyer of the Motel was very French and felt like my heart was going to skip a beat. There was a young Parisian girl at the reception desk. She had beautiful long dark hair with a bounce. She looked at me and said,

"Bonjour Madame, welcome." she clicked away at her computer to bring up my reservation details, I looked around the place in absolute awe. Then the young lady informed me that in was a public holiday for the people and everything is closed today! She then continued to tell me in the most elegant French accent that my room won't be ready until 2pm. OMG! I had to decide what was best for me, Should I take my insulin before I eat? Nothing was opened. I conceded to leave my luggage at the motel and go for a wander to sightsee until my room was ready. Lesson no. 2 check prior if a public holiday, which should have been known by the travel agent. Anyway I should have had something to eat at the airport. I located a little mini market type store, not exactly a 'woolies' store but I had a look anyway. I had previously checked prices in euros so I had an idea. Finally came out with a pack of Cappuccino sachets, 3 bananas and a fresh Baguette.

Walking back to the motel took a bit of navigating, the buildings were so incredible, so old and historic, somehow managed to find my street, 'Rue De Saussure Paris. The street itself was narrow, concrete and cars were parked either side regardless if they were supposed to, it reminded me of Tetris. If your car fits in any space at any angle, well yes you can park it.

"Bonjour Madame" the young receptionist greeted me as I came through the main entry. I smiled back at her, "Bonjour" I replied and was pleased to hear she had my room ready. Taking the elevator to the 3rd floor, room 35, as I glanced around the lift which was small but elegantly furnished in gold and red velvet making a welcoming statement. Arriving on level 3, looking cautiously out the lift doors I see a staircase. Oh dear, only about 10 steps so began my climb dragging my suitcase up each step. I made it to Room 35. My Parisian home for 3 days. The interior of the room was similar to the lift, gold and red. There was a tiny area which I assumed was the kitchenette. I saw a microwave, kettle and tiny fridge and not to mention a sink. Turning to my right was a bar type of bench with two bar stools. How quaint, the dining area? Next to that was a built in wardrobe with no doors but had a nice curtain across it. Looking over the bed which I might add was a sofa bed, the window curtains matched the wardrobe curtains.

Looking further was the bathroom, this clearly was my favourite room. The window was doubled doored, white timber strips and what a view! All the beautiful houses and apartments across the road. First exposure to the French life. The rest of the bathroom was brilliant white, the vanity, toilet and shower. The towels and linen were all the same brilliant white. I loved everything. I wondered what time it would be in Australia, if it was 1245pm in Paris it should be 2215pm in Adelaide. After a rejuvenating shower with French soap and flowery smelling shampoo, I wrapped myself in one of those white fluffy bath towels and collapsed on the bed. It was only then doing I notice the quilt cover was in fact two white sheets sewn together. well I just thought that was different at the time. The bed was comfy and the jetlag must have caught up with me, I woke up an hour later. Feeling refreshed and hungry I got dressed and went for another wander around Paris but in the opposite direction. I was definitely needing a hot meal.

Walking up the main street there were not many people about. I noticed a railway line across the road, didn't see any signs but it went into a tunnel and cars went over the top. There was a news agency which also was a mini mart on the corner but was closed. Exploring the streets, I found the Metro Railway Station. Had no idea where it was going. On my right there was a welcoming aroma of the Pizza shop with tables and chairs outside and every table had an ashtray! Now that's something you wouldn't see in Australia. Apparently there were ashtrays everywhere outside shops, pubs. Entering the Pizza shop I noticed a couple of men and a young boy sitting at a table, no pizza just some drinks. I was greeted by a young French lady who started talking quickly in French, I smiled and told her I was from Australia and my first day. She showed me the menu … ash all in French. I pondered for a moment as I could read French better that understanding the French talking. Sounds odd but got me through and ordered the ham cheese and pineapple pizza. She took my order and while I was waiting at a table the walls were full of prints and posters of New York, yellow taxis, and American collectables. I wasn't interested in New York myself, but found it interesting to find so many in a French pizza place.

I mentioned to the lady when she brought my order over that in Australia my house has many French items and prints. She gave me a free garlic bread, which was as big as the pizza plus it was round and a can of coke! I thanked her and made my way back to the motel, hoping I could find it, turning right I saw my street! Back at Pavilion Carcelle's Marceau. The concierge had changed and he was a large tubby man behind the desk.

"Bonjour" I said as I headed for the lift to the 3rd floor to my room. Practically skipping up the ten steps with anticipation of my pizza. The feeling inside was pure butterflies and this was the best time of my life. My ex and I had often talked about travelling around Europe when he retired from the RAAF, but it's just me and my adventure. Once inside I opened the boxes, and everything looked and smelled amazing! The garlic and cheese were melted right through, so delicious. Taking my insulin, turning on the TV, and flicking through a few channels, settled on a soap opera like The Bold and the Beautiful but a French version. Sitting on the bed all set up to devour my meal. The TV had subtitles but none were in English, I thought that was odd. It wasn't long before I worked out what was going on. Tea was done, I was full after two slices and half the garlic bread, rinsed down with my free Coke. Opening my windows to let the warm afternoon sun come shining through I checked my watch it was 4.15pm, Paris time was 18.45pm so the time in Adelaide, Australia would be 4.15 am not PM. I suddenly felt tired and no way was I intending to go out again this evening I decided to jump into bed and watch TV. All French, even the news but I could make out generally what was happening. It didn't take long before I fell asleep.

Waking up at 10.45pm which would have been 8.15am in Adelaide. I tried to get back to sleep but it took a couple of hours to get centered again. By 5am I was awake and hungry. I made a cappuccino, heated a slice of pizza in the microwave and pigged out on the bed. By the time I had a shower, watched some more French news, dressed and did my hair it was 7am. The full breakfast buffet would be ready by 7.30am. think I had a cat nap as I woke up at 7.23am. Ok time to get my walking shoes on, white tennis shoes, for the big walk around Paris to explore its interesting monuments. Heading downstairs to the breakfast room which was a tiny narrow stairway, unlit and felt like a hobbit's cave I was the first one there. Happily, the actual breakfast room was amazing with benches showcasing various breakfasts treats, yogurts, meats, egg done in many ways, toast and a wonderful coffee machine. The fridge held many types of juices, milks, butters and many cheeses! I made a beeline for the fresh Pastries and Croissants and packed a few in my travel bag for my walk around Paris. Juices and yogurts and of course a Baguette and a banana. That should keep me out of trouble for the day. As I was going to have a coffee I couldn't see any cups or mugs, and yet there were plenty of sugars and teabag varieties.

Oh on the tables all set up, glasses as well for juices. So now I was set up with this amazing breakfast of two cappuccinos, strawberry yogurt, bowl of cereal, toast with honey and also unashamed to admit, two chocolate Croissants. I had enough food and snacks in my travel bag to last me today. Back upstairs to my room I sorted out my blue Rodeo Drive handbag to my smaller blue shoulder bag that keeps things close to my body. No pick pocket thieves today. My passport also fitted inside for safety. I counted my euros, 300, well I set off to see how much damage I could do with that! Hadn't touched anything on my Travel money cards yet.

First item for the day was to locate a post office to purchase a pre-paid international phone card so I can call my sister, Wayne and aunt Mavis in Germany. I could hardly believe I was in Paris. Wishing I had someone with me to share this moment. I had dreamt of being in Paris since I was 14 years old and learning French at school. Thinking of my dad and how we used to talk in French to each other, he would have been so proud of me today. My mum would be too. So I locked my door, skipped down the stairs to the lift to explore! the young lady was behind the reception area again and with a "Bonjour !" and a smile I was out the door. She actually could speak English quite well but we had been conversing in French already, so kept it going. My heart was beating faster than normal with just pure excitement. I went investigating the local shops and little street markets, discovered my local Bakery which wasn't that far from the motel, so this became my morning coffee and Croissant daily shop. This bakery had so many varieties of Croissants that it was difficult to choose. Oh well let's try them all one day at a time. I saw a huge store called MONOPRIX reminded me of MYERS or Target so much to choose from but not as expensive. The streets were coming alive with all the shop owners opening their doors and taking the products outside on the footpaths and some spread out to the streets. The atmosphere was buzzing with activity, friendly people and I even saw a black and white cat, so I took a photo of him.

Wooden boxes filled the paths and produce like fruit, vegetables, bottles of olive oil and cooking spices were all on display. The aroma of coffee stalls, bakery items, and fresh pies was making me hungry. Breads, rolls and so many Baguettes were out for sale. Customers came from everywhere bustling up and down to get their daily needs. Perhaps after the public holiday they may have needed to replenish the pantry. I spent almost an hour in the street market, looking at everything! Some people were selling shoes and handbags. Am sure they saw me coming, I brought a handbag and a purse. 6 euros, I think that was a good price. Lots of stores and stalls up and down the street. Wandering further around the streets of Paris I came to the Metro train station again. Many people going this way and that, in a hurry, like New York Central. I studied the culture of the city people and I really liked the way the men (fathers) took their children to school. 50% share in all the childcare. The women collected the children after school, seemed a fair deal. All the children were dressed in lovely coats, double breasted and a Beret. Reminded me of that show from years ago 'Madeleine'. As yesterday being a public holiday the only people on the streets were putting out recycling and rubbish and there were a couple of people collecting some of the recycling, which seemed fair to me. After mastering the bonjour and bonsoir I was proud of myself for understanding the shop door notices of the days opening hours. Guess learning French at St. Mary's College paid off.

I had walked a lot that day, it was hot about 29 degrees, the paths and streets were all concrete and hilly. Finding the post office to purchase the international sim for 10euros. After having difficulty in getting the sim out of the packaging I needed to go down the street to get a pair of scissors to cut it open which drove me crazy. It didn't fit and didn't work. So just rang Wayne and my sister and took the chance of roaming fees. By the time I had walked around one side of Paris to the side and stopping at every souvenir place for my grandchildren and family, it was almost tea time. I really needed to get back to the motel and not sure which way it was and started walking towards landmarks, the Metro, the Post Office, some magnificent buildings and then I saw the street markets packing up. I knew I wasn't far from my motel! Home at last. Throwing all my shopping onto the bed, which room service had remade and put fresh towels, mats and face washers out. How lovely. The souvenirs consisted of Eiffel Tower keyrings, cards, French designer clothing and calico bags. I had found some French-designed jeweler that I thought would be perfect for one of my granddaughters, Georgia. Oh how I wished I had both Georgia and Imogen with me, we would shop till we dropped. Time for a cuppa and for tea I had the Baguette with banana. There were some waffles with chocolate on them, which I later found out was Nutella. Everything in France had Nutella on it or in it. After walking all day around the concrete footpaths on slopes in Paris, I could see why the French women were not fat from too much Nutella in the diet, you walked off the calories! Considering the cream and butter in most bakery foods, my blood glucose levels were pretty good.

Hot steamy shower, PJs on and French TV, now time to relax. The sun was still up at 9pm and got a bit confused so rang my friend Lisa and Wayne and posted some photos of the inaugural trip around Paris on Facebook. Getting tired I stretched out on the bed, I reflected on the flights over. China Southern upgrading my ticket, feeling very important and served some healthy and delicious meals and the Aircrew were polite and friendly. Air France was a little disappointing. The meals were a delightful cuisine of French dishes plus of course the baskets of Croissants. I managed to watch my French soap show before falling asleep.

Chapter 11:
Paris Landmarks & The Eurostar.

It is Wednesday and tomorrow I go to London. Wow it's just wonderful to wake up in Paris in summer. I started repacking and repacking again for London. Clearly, I need a month to appreciate all of Paris. I wanted to go to the Moulin Rouge show. It didn't start till late at night and I didn't want to roam around loose in the city of Paris. Perhaps in my 20s or even 40s, it would not have worried me being on my own. Heading down to the 'Hobbits' breakfast buffet to replenish myself and the aroma of real coffee was calling my name. Eyeing off all the delights displayed on the counters and in the fridges, the fresh fruit bowls, custards, and yogurts made me hungry. I gathered my healthy supplies for the day, including cold juices as it was getting hot around town. Today I actually walked forever, seeking the ARC de Triomphe. I found it and stood in awe of it. Went inside, read everything, and took photos. On the way back I discovered this souvenir place. It had so many unusual gifts. 115 euros later I was happy. Across the street was the currency exchange place so I thought I'd better get some British pounds for tomorrow. For a while, I just walked around until I found this Parisian Restaurant and thought why not go in style, so I went in and ordered something I had not heard of and they don't have photos on the menu but I took a chance. It looked delicious when she brought it out, reminded me of a Caesar Salad. The egg was on top perfectly rounded and soft. Underneath I could see lettuce, avocado, bacon with cheese or something white. I got a shock when I took a bite of the egg. Oh my goodness it was cold! Not a nice sensation. The cappuccino I had ordered turned out to be black coffee and only half a cup. I think it was like a Turkish coffee. I consumed it all. Thinking along the lines of getting something a little sweeter, I ordered a Chocolate Mousse. It was intense. Death by Chocolate!!

Back in my room, getting into comfortable PJs checking out the plethora of souvenirs and clothes purchased today. Think I may need to post some things back to Australia or get another suitcase. I sassed out what I need to take to London, including my passport, tickets and cash. The plan was to get to the Metro train station to Villiers and then train to Gord de Nord, all organized, all sorted. Sleep time wasn't that easy. I woke at 4am with a pain in the gut. Toilet quickly!! Had a well needed shower and disposed of those granny knickers. Took an Imodium and a Panadeine Forte with a cuppa. Got dressed and laid on the bed and watched something on TV which I thought was R rated. Gradually my tummy settled down and I believe the 'death by chocolate' was the culprit. I just hoped it doesn't happen on the walk to the Metro. So better take another Imodium before I go.

Checking out was slightly daunting, trying to locate where and what train to catch to the Nord International Rail. Yes it all sounded well organized last night, all civilized, today was a different day. I walked up to the Villiers Metro underground carrying a blue suitcase, bags and a large blue handbag, and a large calico bag which had all the souvenirs. Down 3 lots of stairs, got my Metro ticket, but couldn't see Nord on the list of stops, so went back to the ticket window carrying all my luggage.

"Excuse en moi" I said to the ticket man, he was very helpful by walking me to the ticket machine.

"One Nord Billet" he pressed on the screen to 'English' then pressed on 'La Shapelle' and 'one way'. Amazingly I got the ticket. I smiled at him and said

"Merci bien" he smiled back as if to say "Oh my God, these tourists!" going though the ticket entry putting my ticket in and it popped back out as the gates opened. I quickly dragged myself and all my luggage before it closed. Once on the platform I had no idea where I was going. Checking the poster on the wall of the train networks I saw La Shapelle, oh I see now, get off at La Shapelle and walk to Gard de Nord International. Oh yeah easy as mud. A train came in 4 minutes, got on, and watched the flashing lights when approaching the next station. Counting 3 stations to go, with French announcements at each station. Yes, I did think of Shapelle Corby. Ha-ha Aussie humor.

Once off the train dragging my belongings behind me I noticed 3 lots of stairs going up and 2 lots of stairs going down. It seemed like 20 minutes later I was amongst an underground playground. Keeping aware of my surroundings there were many young African men shouting and walking in large groups, not sure if they were going somewhere or just hanging around. This place was scary. Finally, I found exit/entry signs for trains. Suburn and Grande Main signs lit up, and I gathered that 'Grande Main' was my entry. OMG three escalators later I finally reached the Eurostar to London staircase with only 1000 passengers scrambling to get up the stairs. My suitcase and all my bags were becoming heavy, my arms were aching and I was hungry. Persevering up the stairs with people pushing and shoving, like they were catching the last train out of Sydney, another Aussie joke. I got to the top, sweating and really hungry, and was met by the Police!! What a stupid place to check people so very inconvenient. Needed passport and ticket. Showed them my documents then had to go through Border Police (UK). One of the Border Police checking my ticket asked,

"Why you go to London for short time, business or pleasure?" I explained it was first trip, on holidays from Australia. He stamped my passport then firmly said,

"Be careful travelling alone! I took a big breath as I felt I was going to pass out then more police and Customs were needing to check everything! Holy Hell, I had to go through the security screen twice and two Customs officers spoke to another officer quietly and then inspected my second handbag and enquired if it was mine.

"Qui" I replied with a quiver in my voice. All my belongings had to go through another scanner. Hanging tightly onto my passport as in CDG airport the Police took it off me and I had to chase them to get it back. This was totally doing my head in, keeping my eyes on every thing happening. At last I was allowed through. There was a really nice café where I certainly got a strong coffee, from memory I think I had two! I bought a newspaper and a Croissant. Sitting there you were allowed to watch the many Eurostar trains come in and out but NO going on the platform unless it is your train. This is an International center!

Finally, on the Eurostar and time to breathe and relax. Inspector Perot is not going to arrest anyone. I hope anyway. We were going through a tunnel, everything went black and for a moment there I panicked until we went through it and the lights were on. I may have had a snooze, but I walked around to check out this extremely fast train. There was free WIFI, movies and a buffet carriage. Going back to my seat I thought I would have another snooze as I had been up since 4am. Next thing I knew we had arrived in St. Pancreas International Rail. My phone read 10.15am, London was 30 minutes behind I think. Finding the Information desk, told to go to Queens Park Station via Bakers Street line. Did all that and after walking down the main street looking for my motel but there were no signs. I went into a Police station, thought I would ask a 'bobby' where it is, or where to go at least. I waited at least 15 minutes' no one talked to me, despite me standing at the counter. I left and went back to the railway station. The station master kindly informed me that I am in the wrong 'Borough' and going the wrong way.

"You need to go back to Paddington Station then go over the line to Bayswater Station.". So I did that, he was so helpful. at Bayswater Station a tall African man with a wide smiling face, took me to a large billboard map, located exactly where I needed to go.

"Here it is Madame, the motel in just over the next street. Go down here and turn left on Bayswater Road and then left and you will see 'Queens Park Motel". He indicated where it was, only a short distance. I thought ok, I can walk that.

"Thank you so much." I gathered all my luggage and just then started to rain and it was cold. Welcome to London. I wasted nearly two hours and way too tired to see the Silver Vaults that Diana suggested, and no one knew how to get there by public transport. I checked into the motel. I was absolutely speechless. This building looked so grand and luxurious. Fanciest one I've ever been in I think. Settling into my room, was smaller than I thought it would be, but fine for one guest, a single bed and the bathroom was a lovely shade of apricot with apricot luxury towels. On the desk there was an iPad or something like a phone on a charging plate. Apparently you can log on with your room number and find any place you want, and take it with you. How handy was that!

The room was very modern, until I opened the curtains to be greeted by a solid brick wall like 10 inches away from the window, which didn't open. There was air conditioning at least, so closed the curtain. What a surprise when I turn on the TV after I worked out the remote, Neighbors was on! In English, I could listen and not have to translate in my head. I felt right at home. From downstairs I could see the actual 'Queens Park' across the road. Imagine the Queen just living basically across the road! My mum would be so proud. That was a breathtaking moment for me. I unpacked and had a shower then made coffee from the complimentary beverage tray. Venturing out to look for more souvenirs for grandchildren and family. As it was getting close to teatime, well my food and diet had been all over the place since leaving Australia, but I did try to keep to lunch and dinner as best I could due to the insulin injections breakfast and dinner. I thought I would try this restaurant that had fish and chips, to see what all the fuss was about. Well it was filling but nothing to write home about. The fish was lightly battered and the chips were pale. The waiter was very pleasant and kept coming over checking if I needed anything else. Mind you, apart from one couple, I was the only customer. I was really sleepy and looking forward to getting into my bed.

Back in my luxury room in Queens Park Motel I threw everything on the bed and began sorting out clothes and all the gifts I had bought everyone. Looking at it all sprawled over the bed, I knew I had to get another suitcase or zip up tote bag before returning to Australia. After this mammoth task it was definitely time to relax in bed and watch a little TV before shut eye. My travel documents had been sorted for the last leg of my trip. The Eurostar ticket and passport into my small blue bag with the body strap along with my money. Making another coffee and devouring a naughty Nutella waffle which I had purchased in Paris, rich in flavor but as I walked everywhere it wasn't affecting my glucose levels. Slept well, woke about 7am UK time ready for the complimentary breakfast. This dining room was amazing! Top notch and you could have whatever you wanted, hot cooked breakfast eggs done scrambled, poached or fried. Such a gourmet selection and every type of breads and toast, of course I had an English muffin. Sausages, bacon just about anything you could eat was there. Several large Bain Maree all along and around the server, chefs with white hats serving you. Again this reminded me of living in the nurse's quarters. Luxury on steroids. So my 'diabetic' breakfast diet consisted of two poached eggs on thick toast with crispy bacon and a small gourmet sausage. After managing all that I devoured an English muffin with real full on strawberry jam and a large cappuccino. for my travels I packed a yogurt, a banana, an orange, some fancy bread rolls with butter. Fitted into my handbag perfectly, on the way out I grabbed an orange juice and added it to my stash. Checked out and went sightseeing around London.

Not sure how to get to St. Pancreas from the motel, but went for a wander through the park. I saw a horse and carriage coming out of the Queens Gate and 3 ER black royal cars. Was that Harry? Would have loved to have formally met him. Later on I saw a double decker bus near a bus stop so I just hopped on. Unfortunately the driver didn't take cash but he did take MasterCard … how odd and wondered what the fare would be? So used my MasterCard turns out was only 1.83 pounds. Originally I sat up top with bird's eye view but moved downstairs when it started to rain. I was simply amazed at all the places I saw and taking photos of everything, like the Disney Store, Royal Guards. Sometimes I felt like I was going around the Monopoly Board! The sights were just so surreal. Arrived at St. Pancreas International Rail earlier than expected, so browsed around the stores and found a specialty book store with all the famous children's books. I had to get Caroline her first book from London, Peter Rabbit. Next door to that shop was a London jeweler where I purchased a lovely and unusual pair of Pearl earrings, still have them and wear them. A double pearl set. In Paris

I had lost one of my pearl drop earrings, so this was to replace them. That's my story and sticking to that version. Am always losing one earring.

At lunch I met up with some Canadian girls who were travelling to Ireland and UK and were on their way to Paris. To be young and travelling the world, I should have done this many years ago. But never regret having my children, if I had the money I would have taken all three of them abroad, just us. I could have nursed in London hospitals. Once on the Eurostar again, I went for a nanny nap. Bag secured across my body. I woke up in Paris. I went to collect my blue suitcase from the luggage rack at the end of my carriage and noticed it had been moved to the opposite side and two larger suitcases were in its place. At the time I thought nothing of it as my case was smaller and probably moved to accommodate the larger suitcases. Grabbing my luggage and went to the exit, usual Border police and same checking of passport. I asked at the ticket entry.

"Where to Dupleix?" to which she replied it was 'line 6'. Quickly looking around I could only see lines 3, 4 and 5. No line 6. Was getting a bit anxious and of course needing the loo. Unfortunately, there were hundreds of people waiting and were unisex toilets that stunk plus you had to pay to use! Ok let's try and hold on a little longer. I jumped onto the train at Metro 4 line but had to get off a couple of stations as I realized I was going the wrong way.. oh hell what a day. I needed to ask again and was told,

"Go to Metro 4 but change and go Metro 6." I honestly don't know how I did it, no food no drink struggling with all my luggage and two carry bags full of souvenirs and faced with five, yes 5 lots of 20 stairs. Finally arrived at Dupleix station. By the time I walked to the right street I was feeling very unwell, breathless and dehydrated. Not to mention, desperate now to go to the toilet.

Walking from the station to Rue de Viala was only a few meters away. Continued all the way down the street and found the motel. By this time, it was almost 7pm and needing to take my insulin and eat something. The motel looked lovely and proceeded to check in. OMG where are my accommodation documents, my airplane tickets? Gone! That was it I thought I was definitely going to collapse. The time was 7.20pm. Not eaten since London. I have lost them, or been stolen on the Eurostar. Another lesson… keep luggage with you at all times. Looking like a crazy woman I said to the Concierge. "Gone" and shrugged my shoulders in despair. I gave him my passport.

"Ok Madame have info here." He gestured to his computer. I was by this time extremely frantic and felt nauseated. He could tell I was upset and handed me my room key. Room 314.

"Merci Bien." I thanked him and took the elevator to my room. Once inside I threw everything onto the bed, ripping every little thing apart to find my documents. Nowhere. In my panic I called my sister in Australia, apparently it was 3am in Adelaide. I told her of my dilemma, even though I knew she couldn't help but sure felt good to be talking to her, I was, in fact, in another country on the other side of the world, all alone and was a little bit freaked out. Thankfully she calmed me down and I started thinking how I was going to sort this out!

Before I left Australia I had sent my travel information to my eldest son in Queensland Australia, a copy sent from my phone in case anything happened to me overseas. Brad was the executor in my will. I checked my photo gallery on the phone, yes there it was, the code and password information. At least I could breathe a little easier. I finally went to the bathroom before I worked out what I was going to say to the Concierge. Sitting on my bed with chaos all around me, I wrote down in my best French, on this tiny piece of paper, which I think I kept,

"Assister a Peru Aero plane billets, computer imprinted, complaint pour vows euros. Merci been." So off I went and said this to the Concierge. He smiled and knew exactly what was wrong. He replied,

"Yes Madame, enjoy Paris and cruise, relax. Come back in an hour and I will print it out."

He was very comforting and reassuring and he appreciated the fact that I spoke any French at all. He said Well done. Thank you again St. Mary's College.

I went for a walk to buy a coffee and amazingly in this beautiful city, I could not find one. Having settled for a banana and Diet Coke. I walked across the main road where I had disembarked at the train station towards the Eiffel Tower. It was an amazing feeling, absolutely breathtaking sitting there and suddenly feeling homesick. Missing everyone and wishing someone were here to share this moment with me. I could have sat there staring at the Eiffel Tower for ages. The sun was going down and it was time to get back. Bonsoir Paris, I will see you in the morning. Returning to the Concierge I gave him my details, within a few moments I had my whole documentation in my hand. Tickets and accommodation, so very grateful. He would not accept any euros for the printing. Wow how nice. He also made me the best cappuccino I had for a very long time. I slept very well that night. My glucose level was fine and all was well again. I felt bad for waking my sister up in middle of her night. She forgave me, we're sisters. Thank God for that.

Waking up about 5am in Paris, a beautiful summers day. Showered and dressed ready for my buffet breakfast. Today I planned to go on my River Seine Cruise. The breakfast was again a smorgasbord of gourmet delights. As usual I packed a Baguette and banana and a fresh chocolate Croissant. Walking towards the Eiffel Tower, I noticed the Australian Embassy, good to know if I lose anything else. Such an interesting stroll up to the River Seine, passing the Eiffel Tower and the Tennis Court that had the sign up for the Olympic Games and took a photo of it. A lot elder and interesting buildings, gold statues on the Bridge. I took photos of the Carousel that reminded me of my nana merry go round with little horses on it and when it was wound up, it turned and music played. I would love to take Caroline on this ride in Paris. It was busy with lots of children and tourists. Wishing my granddaughters were all here with me to enjoy all this Parisian life. There were tourists beginning to rock up for the cruises. The Eiffel Tower looked so tall and people were waiting at the gate to enter this magnificent structure. I was headstrong on doing this cruise.

It was a Saturday morning about 8am and the ticket office for the cruises didn't open till 9am, strolling along the wharf there were shops, cafes and souvenir shops along the embankment. Restaurants were beginning to cook with some amazing aromas emitting from the kitchens. The main things I noticed sitting on a wooden seat, the French men were out and about on their bicycles or jogging and had their children with them. Giving the mothers to do whatever on a Saturday morning. An American couple sat down beside me to wait for their cruise ticket. They realized straight away I was Australian and vice versa as soon as they spoke I detected their accent also. They told me they had been to Australia, visiting Sydney and Queensland and loved it. Apparently they were in Paris for two weeks after exploring Ireland and the UK. We chatted for a while then I noticed the ticket machines where you could buy your cruise ticket. 15 euros! Perfect deal, people were beginning to queue up as boats began to dock for the cruises. Showing the guy my ticket he ushered me to another pier for my cruise. My cruise liner was bigger than the others, awesome. I boarded the boat and went up to the top deck to soak in the atmosphere. The lady on the cruise crew was giving her tour talk in French as we went around the all the wonderful buildings, explaining when they were built and it was impressive to hear that the Gold statues on the Bridge were donated to Paris by Russia when France became its own country. Couldn't imagine that happening today with countries like America.

I thoroughly enjoyed the cruise down the River Seine and when I went downstairs to check out the view from there I noticed the hand controls with every seat, you could turn the button and you could hear the tour guide in different languages, so handy for different tourists. Being cheeky and in a great mood I was listening to the French version and translating it into English, I so wished my dad was here, we would have had a ball in Paris. The French music started and I recorded it on my phone, took lots of videos and photos. I helped myself to a complimentary coffee and Croissant. After leaving the cruise I headed straight for the souvenir shop on the pier, keeping in mind of luggage and how much was allowable on the plane. Spotting a machine that sold monumental coins of the Eiffel Tower, Arc de Trompe and other interesting places. I chose Eiffel Towers, one for me and one for miss Caroline. Spending an hour at least in the gift shop I had to buy another tote bag to carry it all in. A lovely colorful PARIS tote with a zip and pockets caught my eye, another must have. Perfect. So now I have two full tote bags of souvenirs to carry on the trek back to my motel, The Beaugrenelle Tour Eiffel with the helpful Concierge. There were many African people selling souvenirs on the footpath, one lady wanted a donation for some charity, she followed me, hustled me for ten minutes to get rid of her I offered her 5 euros, she demanded 10 euros saw I had it in my purse and bold as brass took it out and ran! Another lesson learnt.

I was wondering what to have for lunch on my way back, I passed a restaurant that looked like a fancy pub. There were tables out on the sidewalk with as usual ashtrays on them, I was not a smoker at the time so was an ex-smoker but amazed me that nearly everyone smoked. Thinking why aren't these people dying of lung cancer? On researching stats on different countries, yes Europe, especially France had one of the top countries for Lung cancer deaths. So there you go. As an ex-smoker- nonsmoker I chose to sit outside for my meal. Had a chicken dish with a really healthy salad. Definitely not like our Australian salads, nice taste just different. I noticed on my way back after lunch the stores were like David Jones or Myers more high end shoppers. As I turned the corner on my last stretched home, I could smell some beautiful fragrances. I had to go in, I forgot the name but they produce their own French perfumes. They also have a little lab down the back where you can design your own perfumes for 200 euros! I had a sniff at everything and it all smelt the same by the time I had finished. I was really interested in the new Julia Roberts perfume. I purchased a boxed selection of miniature bottles of various French perfumes. Finally a gift for me. ha ha.

The sun was hot, about 28 degrees managing to get a tan. Arrived at the motel exhausted by 3pm. Guess it would be about midnight in Adelaide.

Chapter 11:
Last day in Paris – Au revoir

It was 8pm when I woke up, couldn't believe I had slept through tea time. Looking for something quick I had a cheese sandwich and a coffee. The lunch I had at the pub restaurant filled me up so something light would be perfect. Of course for supper I had one of my cappuccino sachets and a chocolate Croissant that was left over from my trip today. Watched a little of my French soap show and began the arduous task of sorting all my stuff out, everything, last day in Paris. How sad, have loved my time here, loved the culture, the food everything. To be honest I really wanted to stay longer, travel to the countryside of France. Looking at all the things on my bed, clearly I will need to write a list of who is getting what. Yes, I may have overdone the shopping for souvenirs and seriously don't think I will get through the weight at the CDG airport, but I can try. I thought that I could stash shampoos and toiletries into my blue Rodeo Drive handbag. Clothes and medications can go in my blue suitcase. Oh dear I have too much to pack. Looking at my documents I need to put them somewhere very safe, as I just can't go through that scenario again. I checked all my travel documents with time of departure, to China and then home to Australia. Wow it's been nearly 10 days, 3 countries and lots of memories that no one can take from me, or deny me this pleasure trip of a lifetime.

My outbound flight from Paris to China was at 11pm, my motel checks out time was 10am. So filling in the time on my last day would need careful planning. I knew I didn't want to be wandering the streets at night or roaming around waiting for my 'airport transfer' that I had pre-paid and got ripped off. No this time I will need to be organized. On the way back from breakfast I noticed some pamphlets on a wire rack. Airport Direct it says on the cover. A bus that collects passengers going to the airport. 17 euros. Perfect and the pickup points were on the back. What a great idea another lesson to remember next time, don't pay your transfers as more than likely get a slick taxi driver saying he's your Uber transfer guy, but he won't be at all! I tried to call the number but it didn't work and wondered if it was phone, anyway the pamphlet had pick up points dotted on a map. Lucky I was not far from one. No booking needed just hop on hop off, the Airport Coaches leave every two hours. That was the plan for Sunday 11th June, Au revoir Paris. Sightseeing in the morning after breakfast, check out of motel and take all my luggage or rather baggage with me. I thought of getting a trolley, didn't want to look like a homeless French woman!

I enjoyed an enormous breakfast at 7am, Croissant, roll with jam, orange juice and a bowl of coco pops. A large coffee and some cheese to snack on later. Going back to my room I fell asleep till

9am. I still felt tired but knew I could sleep on the plane tonight. Packed my bags for the last time, realizing a ton of feathers is the same as a ton of bricks. If it weighs over the limit, it is OVER the limit. Too late now, just don't go buying anything else. There were some British pounds left in my purse so exchanged them for euros and buy lunch somewhere near the Eiffel Tower. My airport direct bus stop was number 19 at Rue de Suffering which was right next door to the Eiffel Tower. So I checked out of Beaugrenelles Tour Eiffel thanking the Concierge for his assistance with the computer. I slowly started to walk towards the high end shops to where the airport bus stop was nearby. It only took 5 minutes to walk there and there was a bus waiting, what luck the driver spoke French but I just gave him the 17 euros and said 'airport' and a young African chap jumped out, grabbed my suitcase and put it in the rear luggage compartment. I tried to object but he kept saying it was his job, all good, very safe. Well I don't think I took a breath for the first 20 minutes on that ride. The other passengers were very calm and relaxed so I settled down and enjoyed the tour through the rest of Paris to the CDG Airport. Going through the tunnel again, thinking of Lady Diana. I was pleased that I had all my personal papers on me, not taking any chances. Arrived at CDG Airport and greeted by men with guns, machine guns and dogs, basically all German Shepherds. Spent an hour looking for a machine to print out my boarding pass. Found one with 'English' and required to put my passport in it, I held my breath with every minute and kept my hand on it. It may have disappeared into a hole if so I was going with it. Pressed on 'ticket' and a boarding pass popped out which had my name and details on it. Breathe again, breathe. I then went to the Air France office and confirmed my data on boarding pass. YES! All good to go.

Having decided to have lunch and hopefully somewhere I can recharge my phone so I could contact Wayne and Margaret. The café was extremely busy, I kept forgetting this was an International airport that flies in and out to countries all around the world. I should be making friends with some of these travelers, I did say 'some'. There were those not so friendly from not so friendly countries. I made my way up to the lifts where a security man got out to let me enter and asked me where I was flying to,

"Guangzhou in China, 2E departure, then to Australia." He then pressed the button to the appropriate level. Up we went to my level, I felt trapped in a computer game 'Wolfenstein' my children used to play. The lift door opened and there were several guards, security, Police and military personal all armed with rifles. I found one seat available, there were thousands of international travelers and I was curious where they were all destined. The armed guards walked up and down, some had dogs. I kept thinking 'Don't look them in the eyes, look straight ahead.' The area had an unusual stench about it, not quite sure but it was a smelly dirty feet odor mixed with curry. Not pleasant at all. The worst thing was I needed to go to the toilet, but couldn't leave my seat. My son text me and that made me feel better, less anxious. Missing my family and grandchildren. So many gifts for all of them. I still needed to get some Panda Bears in China.

Gosh I was getting tired, but I couldn't go through customs until 7pm, three hours to go. Reflecting on my holiday, it has been a wonderful trip, and perhaps caught the travel bug with thoughts of returning for at least a month. So far my fractured coccyx has not been too bad, however, sitting long hours on the plane may start the pain. I had been taking one panadeine forte every day. Checking my mobile phone and still had no reply from Queens' Park Motel regarding locating my missing documents. Chatting to my sister Kathy, the little red haired girl, LOL, she was a good sport as it was after midnight in her neck of the woods, in NSW Australia. Kathy kept me awake and definitely entertained. I wish I had taken Kathy on this trip with me. Dad would call us 'Thelma and Louise' when we were going on road trips across the states. Good memories. It seemed weird that my Air France departure was at 1120pm and then at approximately 1220am will be served dinner and at 4pm be served breakfast. At least there were movies, games and sports to watch all night with free headphones. Checking out my old boarding pass to China was seat 42L in Premium section. Plenty of leg room, hot white towels a tote bag with slippers and toiletries inside. Reading the boarding pass the word 'seat' was spelt 'siege', slightly concerning. I was pulling things out of the two extra tote bags I had to buy for all the souvenirs from various parts of the world, well Europe at least. There were special items for friends and of course my family and Wayne. He had been my rock, he loved me enough to let me go on my adventures overseas. I felt relaxed in my heart that we had a good friendship and we were open and honest with each other. Perhaps some things should have remained unsaid, but what's done is done. You can't unheard something you've been told, just like you can't unseen something you have seen.

Once in the departure lounge of CDG airport I headed straight for the Duty Free shop. I purchased a carton of cigarettes for Wayne. I didn't smoke but thought it would be a nice gift and only 48 euros. The chap at the counter informed me I could buy up to two cartons. I thanked him but I hardly had room for this carton. I had already purchased the Julia Roberts perfume, La Vie La Belle. I had my trade mark signature perfume, TABU since the age of 14 years, everyone knew me by that fragrance. So trying a new fragrance was very special. I noticed these beautiful scarfs, one in black and another in pink, with Eiffel Tower print. So I bought one, maybe I could wear it instead of packing it, and where did I think I would pack it anyway. It is now almost 1950hrs, just over 2 hours till I board have noticed many passengers with lots of carryon luggage and many of them with big arises. As I was lining up to go through customs this African lady, large as life waves her baton in my direction and says loudly,

"Madame you must weigh at machine, go to machine, all luggage to weigh now!" she marched over to me and grabbed my bags by force and started weighing everything, even removing my small blue bag with my passport, ticket and money in it. Very aggressive I thought. She continued to go through the calico bag and my PARIS tote, filled to the brim with souvenirs. Waving her baton at me she pointed to another direction way down the other end of the check in.

Well I was not happy Jan, I was over the limit, which yes I kind of knew that, but others had heaps of carry on and had big arises. I ran as fast as I could to check in my suitcase. Just made it, the baggage crew quickly put a tag on it, Adelaide Australia. So my suitcase wasn't going to be with me till I get to Adelaide! I screamed out, trying to grab back my suitcase,

"My drugs are in there, please need my drugs!" immediately four large securities with dogs and pointing their long rifles directly at me. They were telling me to stand back, no touch bag. This was a nightmare. One Customs officer opened my suitcase so I could get 'medications' as I explained, 'Diabetic'. I grabbed my clear bag with my medications and prescriptions and thanked them. I had my insulin. Very quickly they zipped up the suitcase and labelled it again and poof, it was gone. I then had to run like hell back to my boarding gate. Breathless and sweaty I met the African woman again and she had the audacity to weigh my other bags again. Phew! Made it through and no problems checking my passport either. Was hoping that no one puts anything inside my bag, hate to be caught up in some drug smuggling crap. Take a big breath, relax. I heard the overhead announcements saying flights to Dublin, Boston and Moscow. Reminded me again this is an International Airport many hours away from home. Just over 24 hours, being 20 hours flying time, I would be home.

Having a double check in my small blue bag for passport, money and documents, made me realize that my Nurses Registration isn't the only important thing to me, it is now my passport. Thank goodness I didn't lose it in London. Travel smart had recommended taking a photo of it for extra protection, so I did that. Was feeling thirsty and could do with something to snack on, but knowing soon I will give a meal on the plane. OMG where are my insulin needles? Will need to buy four at a pharmacy in Guangzhou airport…. surely there would be a pharmacy. I panicked a bit because I needed them before I ate on the plane. Trying to relax and take my mind off the insulin, I sat there checking the other passengers out, knowing I shouldn't but I did. I did get a laugh or two but some people looked like actors. Like the Sticky Bandits from the Home Alone 2 movie. Katie from the Bold and the Beautiful. It is getting boring now, I need some water to take my Metformin, as I can't take any insulin without needles.

A family just had a loud argument and I was trying to not only not listen but not to laugh. The father had accidently opened the daughters' suitcase and all the contents fell out. All members of the family were yelling at each other in a foreign language. There must be a plane about to take off as 'final boarding 'beams across the PR systems in a few languages, including French, as several passengers are racing like the devil is after them. Absolutely hilarious. I tried to find my Paris coloring book, but it's in my suitcase. Only have the pencils in the Tote bag. Rechecking my bags in case there maybe one or two insulin needles, not sure how long I can go without any insulin. Yes, best go to pharmacy at Guangzhou airport. At least my Diabetes membership card and seniors card are in my purse. Oh bugger have remembered all my prescriptions are in the suitcase and won't get that until Adelaide. I tell myself to relax as I cannot control what I cannot control. I was able to take my Nexium, definitely can't go without that, the reflux pain becomes quite unbearable. Looking around I see passengers buying heaps of food, surely they must realize they are going to get a full meal on the flight.

Recapping on my first overseas trip. Departed Adelaide Australia on a Sunday at 10am. Great flight with an upgrade to Premium. Saw the moon going up in one part and the sun in another.

I went over the Equator. The clouds in China were different viewing from the plane, white clumps like cotton balls on top of each other ascending into the sky. Reminded me of Mr. Whippy ice cream cone or a Macca's cone. My mind came back to the needles, if I could find the snap bag with the used needles I could use one, for an emergency as it was only my needles. No such luck. Perusing through my passport, I have a red stamp from Australia and not sure if it is an extra stamp, I see 5 stamps, maybe 6 if you count the Aussie one. Not feeling well and really need a drink of water, I managed to get a small bottle of coke. After that I just went back to Gate 53 to wait for my Air France flight to Guangzhou. Must have dosed off as next thing I knew we were being called for boarding!

Arrived at Guangzhou finally and sustaining some scary turbulence which I was not impressed with at all. From my window I could see large flashes of lightning and that was freaky. Landing safely and found my way to the International waiting area. There were no signs for Adelaide, Australia. Running to the Aircrew desk to check why, then they informed me that it was too early yet. When time gets closer, it will display. Thank you now let's find the pharmacy. No entry to the main part of airport, I must stay in my gated area. Cricky mate I thought, its medical! Oh well back to the waiting area, two coffees and a horrid tasting hamburger later I found Gate A03. Sitting on my bum for another two hours, took photos of the display when it became available. CZ663 Adelaide

A03 boarding at 2135hs. Currently it was 1943 hrs. so not too long, I had been shopping again just little bits at Chinese souvenir shop.

Finally, on the plane, decided China Southern was the best. Alas I was sitting next to a Japanese man, behind me and one in front. A young woman wanted to swap seats so she could sit near the Japanese man. He did not want to sit next to her and refused to change seats. She made a big fuss and the Co Pilot came down to tell her off and stop this disturbance. So nobody changed seats, we all settled down and of course within an hour we were served our meal and watching a movie. Throughout the flight the Japanese man who was acting strange at the airport, was now causing a disturbance again. demanding bottles of water every hour and was extremely rude to the Crew. I must add when we landed in Adelaide airport, this gentleman was quickly escorted to a private room by AFP and going to be scanned for drugs. Security drug patrol were with them. The flight had been long and I was ready to be home. We were all lined up to be checked by customs, it was only then I noticed up the top level were Customs officers with rifles too. Didn't think we did that, but hey it's our country's security.

The sniffer dogs were stopping at certain people waiting in line. Some actually asked to step out of the line. One dog actually sat and the woman tried to shoo it away. Two Officers immediately yelled not to touch the dogs! She was trying to hit it to go away. She too was taken out of the line and into a room near the Japanese man.

Customs were checking the yellow declaration forms we had to fill out. I looked at mine again, I had the carton of smokes, but no idea if over 50g, Duty Free man said I could take 2 cartons, only had one. So to be on the safe side I changed my NO to a YES. The customs officer shows the form to another person, holding a rifle, and they kept looking at me and looking at the form. One of them came over and asked why did I change it, I explained why and everything was checked. He took the carton opened it and handed me back one packet.

"This is 50g. I will destroy the rest!" so lesson learnt. Now I was pissed off and just wanted to go home…. this is my own country. He wasn't interested in my unopened box of French perfumes, so off I went. Reentering Australia. I was happy to be home and to see my old friends, Lisa, Phil and Wayne. Of course my beautiful cat, Maddie, was very pleased to see me. She purred so loud and snuggled into my neck. The first thing I did was find my needles and had my insulin. I was home.

Chapter 12:
The Road Trip Preparation

Once back from overseas, the relationship and friendship changed with Wayne somehow. Maybe I talked too much about Paris to my friends and family. He was determined to get his own passport and wanted to take me to Hawaii, mind you he would say and promise lots of things that never actually happened. Like when were first met and we would talk about the Crickyet and plan to go and have a beer or two. We never went and I found out he gave up drinking 20 years prior as it was affecting his attitude and created aggressiveness. We never went forward; it was always backwards. He would want to meet my family and grandchildren, but as the years went on, he just wanted to stay home and preferred me to do the same. I was working fulltime and loving my job, and saved heaps to go for trips around Australia visiting family. He did not communicate with his family and if I pressed the subject he would get very angry and aggressive. So after a couple of years just let it go. I planned a few holidays for us, flying interstate, staying in motels, hiring cars. Because he eventually told me he did not have a driver's license, never had one, but I know he drove and had a car registered in his name.

It became a slippery slope of not quite the truth. We did however get along better as housemates rather than a couple. That suited me fine. We shared things like Maddie the cat, when she passed away we were both really affected. About a year later we got a rescue Staffy, which I always say she rescued me. 70% of the time Wayne and I got along well. Introduced him to my dear friend Diana and her partner Daniel. It was really good, until it wasn't. Wayne was declining all social gatherings and for a short time I went alone to visit my friends, usually all nurses that I had worked with for years. I believe he used to dislike it when all my friends would come around to our place for BBQs or parties and started making it obvious. They felt unwelcomed and over the years, they stopped coming to visit. I had a good job and great carerin nursing and worked as secretary for Neighborhood Watch. I had a great relationship with the Police. After a while he told me he had been in trouble with the police, in more than one state of Australia. Eventually I had to resign from my role with SAPOL, just to protect myself.

He applied for his passport and I paid for it. He kept saying he was going to travel here and there and we would have a great time. I worked full time, full on, and earnt a good salary, which we spent on trips and interstate gatherings. Unfortunately for me I began having really bad shoulder pains which eventually required surgery. Then Covid 19 struck, so no non urgent surgeries and no appointments with specialists like Orthopedics to review my painful shoulders that was preventing me from working. Centrelink assessed me once, had a case manager that I saw only the once. due to 'Covid restrictions'. Somehow I thought I would get phone calls at least, not just put on jobseeker allowance! From earning over $2500 per week to $668 per fortnight is was extremely hard on me financially. It was around this time I became depressed. More depressed than usual. No money for bills or food and I was not happy. My life definitely spiraled out of control. Not only was I paying for pain killers, I was so sleepy from the drugs I slept most of the day, when not asleep was in agony from pain.

Wayne had to do most of the house chores whilst I was unable to move. Hanging out washing, vacuuming, showering was so difficult to do as I couldn't raise my arms to wash my hair, dressing and undressing was almost impossible. so required to wear loose sloppy clothes to get around this issue. Due to pain and not in the mood to be social it created a culture of Wayne taking care of me, he had the control. If we argued I would give in just so it would be peaceful. I saw less and less of my friends. Diana and I would talk on the phone and clearly Wayne was annoyed, despite the fact they got along. I became frustrated and felt locked in a cell. Whenever I voiced an opinion or didn't agree with someone Wayne wanted he would carry on and yell and throw himself around stomping and scaring the Staff. This was becoming worse. I couldn't afford to go anywhere, join in with my usual mates in social events and too ashamed to tell anyone he was bullying me around. He would spend his pension on things he really did not need to. But saying no was not an option. The washing machine finally broke down; it had been inherited from my mother before she passed away. Luckily my youngest son was living in the same block of units and was able to wash my big stuff, and I had to wash other stuff by hand in the laundry sink. Now this activity increased the pain in my wrists, Tendonitis and Carpel Tunnel Syndrome. Eventually I had surgery on my left Shoulder and a week later had surgery on my right wrist, Carpal Tunnel Release. All made worse by the wring of clothes by hand.

It was not until after my surgery and post rehabilitation that I noticed any changes. Apart from living like strangers or brother and sister, he was becoming highly aggressive and agitated in general. I always took the brunt of it all. I was physically better post-surgery and I was then eligible for the age pension. He would start telling me what he would like for dinner, how he wants it cooked and things like that. At first it was ok but then it wasn't. things took a curve when I was trying to save to get a washing machine, and he went out and purchased a statue, like a dragon with lady statue for $175! admittedly it was a nice statue, but I needed a washing machine first. I thought that was selfish. This began my anger with him. As long as he got what he wanted, that was ok. Not long after that, belongings became 'his' and 'hers' and this really concerned me. He was becoming very controlling. As I was working I had bought most of the furniture, household items like the fridge and dining suite. But never classed them as his or hers.

During my recovery I was able to do more activity, like hanging the washing out. He would have a hissy fit if I starting doing it, he wanted to be the hero and do it. The more independent I became and wanted to get back to my social life, he would make something up in his head. He was convinced I was having an affair with the guy next door, who Wayne was more friends with than I ever was. The last straw came when he accused me of taking money out of his account, or hiding the money he gave for his share of the rent or food. I had enough of this shit and he kept saying,

"I could just not take my medications and kill the lot of you, anybody who gives me a hard time or rips me off." Now that sounded like a threat and I had to check he had taken his meds. After an argument I thought he was going to hit me. I started telling my son what was happening, to keep an eye on things in case I was killed or injured. I was 67 years of age and was not going to be threatened by anybody. I simply was too old for that. I discretely told my closest friends in case something happens to me. Diana and Daniel offered me to stay with them as long as I wanted or needed. My other mate offered me the same. She was very concerned about my safety.

I told him we had to be adults about this situation. At the time he agreed. So he decided he was going to leave the state, go out bush or country thinking he'll be ok, salvos and housing trust would look after him, and he had his disability pension. He insisted I kept our private arguments private and not to tell people things that he had said or done.

"Let's just be adults and have a peaceful break up, you and the dog stay here, I will go to Wangaratta or out country. I will just take my ornaments and clothes, you have the rest, oh I will collect the large statues later, just pack them for me." So that was his version of breaking up. Book a coach to Albury somewhere, see the Salvos when you get off the coach, and get housing and settled on the 22nd December. I suggested he ring them first as it would be Friday at 5pm just before Christmas eve. Lucky he did, no vacancies, no office open over public holidays and they suggested he stay where he was in SA as there were no rentals or assistance with bonds. He realized he would be homeless, limited food, no cigarettes and this didn't fit right with his plans. He then told me I would have to get out and he was having the Staff.

A huge argument commenced, my son came down to punch him out, believe me it was a scene from Kath n Kim. But no one was laughing, I physically tried to hold my son back as they were having the verbal and almost physical argument. My son showed me his phone, he had 000 showing all he had to do is press. Wayne thought he was calling his cousins for 'back up' and feathers flew! The neighborhood heard it all. After an hour my son went home, I went to my room with the dog, and he sat on his recliner with a crazed look on his face, wide eyed and held onto his baseball bat. Waiting, waiting. This went on for at least two weeks. Every day he would sit there with his baseball bat. Every night he would lay in bed with his baseball bat. During the night he would shout out things so I could hear him, laughing and threatening. I lasted about 4 days before I decided to stay with my friends. No way was I going to 'poke the bear' as I had to pack my things. Sell what I could and organize a storage unit. I had to be strong. My son in Queensland rang every couple of days to see how I was. A bloody nervous wreck actually. I could go down the DV route as I knew all the Community Police and organizations, I was too embarrassed to tell them, I felt foolish. So much more happened and involved with this situation I may be able to talk about it one day, today is not the day.

I rang the landlord to notify him that I was vacating the unit and gave him an end date. It was necessary to keep things quiet as I was trying to find other accommodation. Well the unbelievable happened! within 5 minutes of me calling the landlord, the landlord rang Wayne and told him. They made a time to meet to arrange the changeover on the lease. Since when in this era of DV is it right or safe for people to advise the perpetrator of DV information from the victim. I had to have a backup plan, for my safety. I was really angry with the landlord. Trying to keep the peace I said I was going to spend a few days at my friends. Allowing me to think what to do. My son had already given notice for vacating his unit, so here we were trying to pack and move without starting a riot. Wayne was being an absolute arsehole to me and when I was there moving things into my car to put in storage he kept muttering abuse. The next day moving more stuff, he offered to help me at the storage unit. Declining his offer for obvious reasons, he got really annoyed, he said he doesn't understand why I can't just move back to the retirement place next door and we can share the dog. No way was I going to live next door to this crazy paranoid violent man, who has not enhanced my life at all. I actually detested him for letting my life turn to shit, but then maybe it was my own fault. How did I get to this stage?

Having a meltdown, I went to my friend Diana's. I was safe, I could just be me, and she wouldn't let anyone hurt me. Later that week I told Wayne I was spending Christmas with my son in Queensland and to work himself out as I was done. Of course he apologized in so many ways, trying to work it out so we could stay friends. Things were dark and black for me and nothing was going to change. Michael moved out and resettled, happily he is still resettled. I left my car at Michaels carport for safety. My eldest son was happy to come up for Christmas. Originally Bradley and his family were coming down to SA and had booked a holiday house at

Victor Harbor and all the family, my sister, his cousins were all going to be seeing each other for first time in years for Christmas. As the situation was getting bad with me, the holiday plan was cancelled. This sent my family into a spin and blamed Wayne. I had planned to stay up in Queensland for a few weeks. I was seeing my daughter and the adult grandchildren on Christmas day and was so looking forward to it. Melanie's birthday would be another occasion I wanted to be part of and my granddaughter's 21st. I flew up on the 13th December, two days later I received a phone call from a Neurologist from Flinders Hospital. Wayne had suffered a stroke and was in critical condition. He required urgent and lifesaving surgery. They needed my permission as he was not able to consent himself. I gave permission, however they would need to track down his family for NOK.

This was the beginning of another roller coaster. This went on for weeks. In ICU, deaths door, another procedure on ward then back to ICU. Two days after Christmas I had to fly back to SA, changed my flight, incurring an extra $100. The specialist team and Social worker rang me every day to keep me up to date or ask for consent for another specialized procedure that only certain surgeons could do. I also was contacted by the neighbor in regards to the dog. My darling Flossy, no one could take her to care for her. Diana fed her, took photos, Al next door fed her too. I needed temporary dog career. In the end my friend Derek, my ex's mate, took her for me. That in itself is another story.

I got to speak to Wayne in ICU. He had suffered many strokes and doctors informed me he had Lung cancer, but he has primary somewhere they suspect bowel cancer. Currently they weren't going to investigate as he is still critical and his body keeps shooting of blood clots. So he was very ill and it was touch and go for weeks. He started being aggressive with staff and the doctors preventing them to treat him. He was put into an induced coma for medical reasons. Whenever he was lucid he would try to text me, actually anybody, up to 56 times each. He would say threatening things to people and text outrageous threats. At one point he texts me DEAD, and threatened to pour boiling water over my son. Well nobody gets to threaten my family. I spoke with the social worker explaining he cannot keep calling me or threatening me or my family. He continued for many weeks. I spoke to the social worker and the nurses, but did not go visit him as he continued to threaten me. I blocked him. I lost the dog, my darling Flossy to RSPCA and then rehomed. The doctors say he was good one day and not so good the next. I was staying at Diana's the whole time. They said I was welcome as long as I needed.

I ensured during this time to get any personal items of mine out of the unit and into storage. Each day I was exhausted. I would go back to Diana's at night and watch the Crown series with her again and slept right through the night. She was working at the TAFE teaching, currently on holidays over the Christmas break. We had some good laughs and we enjoyed the time together. Daniel was not having a good time, he had been diagnosed with sorboses of the liver and was on medications. Unfortunately, he continued to drink up to 4L of wine a day. Diana was not happy. Daniel was in denial and kept cancelling his appointments. He continued to work, but limited hours. It was just a mess. Diana really want me to stay longer, and hoped Daniel would go to rehab. The neighbor, Al, kept in touch with Wayne's condition. He was demanded ridiculous items like cigarettes, pot, a lighter and his keycard. Being in ICU the nurses stated he cannot feed himself or walk, he had a feeding tube through his nose to his stomach, he will not be allowed any cigarettes. I gave by text his accounts due to be paid and the social worker assured me she would handle it all with Centrelink. It never happened. The landlord told me that Wayne was in arrears in his rent and so far he would lose his bond with the housing trust. I explained the social worker should be able to sort that out with Wayne as he hadn't spent any money since he had been in hospital. Very good, the Social worker and the landlord are all on the same page. Not my problem. So I thought.

Anyway weeks go on this merry go round. He is going to rehab, still can't walk or eat on his own will need a carerand unable to return to the unit… not my problem. I did feel guilty that I didn't see him in hospital but nurses advised me not to if he is aggressive as he potentially will stroke out again. On a phone call via the neurologist I informed very clearly to Wayne he must tell the staff of his wishes should this happen again. He was quite clear that he wanted treatment, have no idea if he had knowledge of his diagnosis of lung cancer. The doctors told me he had been told. So I wished him well and requested to not call 100 times a day, just to abuse me. Another issue I had with the landlord and I checked into the legality of it for my knowledge and for Wayne. The landlord wanted his arrears rent money, Wayne wanted to keep the unit. Therefore, he had an obligation to pay the rent or he would be homeless. The landlord requested the neighbor get the keycard for him and he, the landlord will take it to Wayne to get the money out or transfer for the rent owed. Now he was in ICU, unable to walk, eat on his own, let alone go to an ATM or Westpac Bank. On the 7th January landlord told me he got his full rent money. I wondered how he did that?

On the 12th January I received an email from the bank, to Wayne in response to his claim 'someone has taken money out of my account', apparently they were investigating re the Fraud Department. Thank God I didn't touch it, but very suspicious of the landlord. I kept getting emails from various debt collectors addressed to Wayne. I emailed him directly to advise him that he must use his own email. It continued for weeks, so I emailed the companies direct. So far so good. A few weeks after that the unit was re rented to new tenants. I still had furniture and personal items inside, I heard Wayne arranged a removals to take a few things he wanted and the landlord took the rest! My dear Diana and her partner helped me with storage of the items I had removed before this all happened. I stayed with Diana for a while, and they were amazing to me. The dog went to be rehomed and I made plans to fly to QLD for Christmas. We held a party for Daniels' 50th and that was a bit rough as he had been unwell with something re his liver. He was on medication. Unfortunately, he couldn't give up the alcohol.

Deciding to give Diana and Daniel a break I drove to the country to visit my cousin, who had been unwell and her husband too was getting on. It was Melbourne Cup day and when I arrived at my cousin's place, a very quaint property with ponies and a fat sheep, we put the TV on to watch the race. We were on the wrong channel, watching the wrong race entirely. Her husband arrived home from the local pub where he had watched the race. He burst out laughing when he found out we had missed the race. Anyway we didn't have a bet on it, so no harm done. I enjoyed spending a few days with her, a bit of serenity away from all the troubles re Wayne and taking in some R and R so to speak. I was lucky enough to catch up with my nieces / cousins with a huge roast dinner and lots of roasted vegetables and country style gravy. It was a wonderful catch up with everyone.

One of my nieces has two young girls, apart from her adult children and these little ones are actually the cutest of all. The youngest about four I think, absolutely gorgeous and so much like her mum as a little girl. Jolene designed and made by hand a lovely Quilt a few years ago, I still have it and is a credit to her. She does quilting and has for years, she is always doing one for somebody. Extremely talented for someone nearly 80 years young. I explained that I was going to pack my car and do a road trip to Queensland via NSW stopping to see my sister and brother, one on the South Coast and the other in the Hunter Valley. It was sad to leave and say goodbye to her, but promised I would come back after I was settled in Old. I left the next morning, ready for the four-hour trip back to Diana's where we had some great nights full of laughter and many discussions about this book. She was so proud of me and we were the best of friends, always will. I packed my little blue car and had food and medications in an sky for the long road trip. Promising Diana, I will definitely be back to visit once I settled. She hugged me so hard I thought she was going to break. As soon as I drove off, I missed her.

Chapter 13 :
The Road Trip.

My first stop apart from fuel and food stops was Balranald Motel. Hot as hell, enjoyed the shower, and after a good meal fell asleep on a fairly comfortable bed. Good price, directly outside was car parking, there was a swimming pool but I didn't use it. The next stop was Wagga Wagga, which was very hot and the Motel was extremely hard to locate. It was a new one in town and I drove two hours trying to find it. I asked anybody on the streets, even road workers and the Police. Totally dehydrated, anxious and hungry, but finally found it tucked away on the top level of a bakery, which was closed. The door was locked, no reception, I called the phone number on the window, no reply. In desperation I walked five shops down and collapsed outside a shop. As it turned out it was an Aged Care Community Centre that were about to close for the day. Two ladies helped me to a chair, one lady got a glass of chilled water for me and after telling them I was a diabetic, the other lady ran to get a packet of biscuits. The water was so refreshing and I very much appreciated the biscuits even though they were plain milk biscuits.

They phoned the Manhattan Motel for me, and an automated voice with instructions was heard. I checked the message on my phone regards to my code to enter including my room number. Thanking these ladies so much I began to walk back to the Manhattan Motel. Using the code I opened the door to be faced with a flight of stairs, there was a lift but of course it wasn't working. After two flights of stairs I found my room. Nice room with a refrigerator for my drinks, food and insulin. There was an enormous bathroom with rails like a disabled facility. The fly screens were broken but there was air conditioning so wasn't bothered too much just left the windows closed. Fell asleep after my shower and dinner. Good night. In the morning I txt my sister in NSW letting her know I would arrive tomorrow and will be staying a couple of days. My first stop was to Moss Vale Cemetery to visit Barrie's grave, then onto the Macquarie Pass windy road that I know so well. Then onto Oak Flats that I also know so well from my childhood to see the little red haired girl! We no longer needed to pretend anymore. We had a wonderful couple of days, belly laughs and my niece and I had a well-earned catch up. Even my nephew made the effort to pop over to see me. It was good for the soul hanging with my family. We ordered Chinese food the night before I left.

Next stop on my long road trip was the Hunter area to visit my brother. We were just as excited as each other to catch up. I stayed for a few days and enjoyed every minute. We too had some great childhood memories to share. It was hard to leave but promised I would be back soon as I settle. I had booked into a motel at Coffs Harbor at some motel, limited parking but had a reception area. Of course this also had stairs to my room. So I bundled my luggage upstairs, then noticed the lift. Dumping everything on the bed I quickly ran across the road to Kmart and Coles, mind you when I say 'ran' it really is a quick walk. Bought some refreshments and food snacks for my last lap of my trip. In Kmart I spotted some really summery shorts and a white ribbed top. It would have been awesome on me 25 years ago I think, but hey it was cool to wear while driving to QLD. The outfit I have worn twice only. Eventually I gave a load of stuff to an op shop in QLD not long ago. Looking around the motel room it was very basic, a queen size bed, a small round stool next to the bed. A small built in robe with no doors, ha ha, reminded me of the Paris room, for some odd reason there was a very small basin or small sick in the corner of the room with one tap, cold water only. The bathrooms were down the hall adjacent to my room. Passing the bathroom I noticed three steps going up to the communal kitchen which had absolutely awesome views of Coffs Harbor. I had to leave my insulins in the communal fridge with my yogurts and chicken meal. I quickly put a label on them, not that I would begrudge a hungry person eating the food, but would be annoyed if someone stole my insulin.

Rearranging my blue suitcase and writing in my notebook for my info from travel stops, fuel usage and motel documentation. Like as if I was doing a travel journal on my road trip, this was going to be final trip in the car. Maybe short trips around Queensland to sightsee or visit my grandson on the Sunshine Coast perhaps. I actually had a good trip despite the extremely hot weather. I had air conditioning and the little Ford Focus did an excellent drive all the way from Adelaide. Plus I didn't get lost even when the Gipson my phone died after the charger ran out and no longer worked. Have since order a new one to match my new IPhone as it apparently has a different USB charging port. I was so very proud to say I found my way safely to my son's waterfront apartment without Siri to help. Arriving at my son's I had a shower and a nanny nap before I emptied my car. My son detailed the car the next week. Fantastic job! Now I only had to settle into my new digs. I stayed indoors all weekend, on the Monday I thought I would venture out to vacuum my car, mainly dog hair from the Staff. I saw the School Zone sign flashing so obviously slowed down, I spotted a Shell service station across the road, so indicated that I was getting into the right lane. Wrong! Motorcycle cop waves me down to pull over. $309.00 later and very apologetic, I returned to the road, headed to the servo. Not a car wash! No vacuuming! Decided it was safer just to go home and tell Brad my sad tale.

In the March, after spending $1,600.00 on getting my car checked and repairs for QLD registration, I decided to take a Greyhound Coach to Newcastle to see my brother, Tom. We spent about a week together, having a great time and even had a wonderful catch up with my step daughter, who I have always felt as a daughter. We all went to the Trivia night at Branxton Golf Club and had tea. We were doing ok in Trivia at first, but after Hayley left to go home, we went downhill! The next night we went to the meat raffles and Tom won twice! A huge tray of Steaks and another tray full of vegetables! We shared them with my nephew and his girlfriend. Absolutely delicious. While it was so great spending time with Tom and his lovable cat Polly and not to forget Chloe, little Jack Russell who I missed so much when I left, I had to check dates in my diary as I had to ensure I flew to Adelaide to see my youngest son and my best friend Diana was having a birthday on the 23rd of March and my other mate had a birthday on the 30th March, so thought I would catch up with her too. A good opportunity to catch up with my youngest sister, this was my plan. The storage shed was also on my agenda to gradually empty and reducing an expense.

Chapter 13 :
The Last Whoo Rah - 140 Days.

Tom and I were having an awesome day out travelling around Maitland when I got a call from Daniel, my darling Diana's partner. I honestly thought he was calling about her upcoming birthday party and my flight plans. Unfortunately, not so. Apparently Diana had fell ill at work and was hospitalized. Holy Hell! There was not a good diagnosis, after scans attended and many specialists involved I heard my heart crack. Cramps twisted in my stomach. Shocked and absolutely devastated for Diana, for Daniel and myself. I have loved her for almost 30 years, such a wonderful friend. Everything went black for me. The diagnosis was Stage 4 NSC Lung Cancer in left lung with metastatic tumor in the right side of her brain, spine and was under 50kg. The treatment plan was to do radiation to the brain tumor, which was 2.5cm. The initial plan was to give her a huge dose to the brain, cerebellum area to reduce the size on the 20th March. She was home waiting for this treatment, trying to process what was happening and being a nurse wondered what the prognosis would be. Two days later her partner had a fall in the bathroom, ambulance rushed him to hospital, straight into ICU for only a few hours. Daniels liver specialist was there when he suffered a massive seizure, went to Palliative Care Ward where he passed away. Diana was so overwhelmed it was just too much for her to handle. I immediately booked a flight and went to SA to be with her. He was cremated, Diana had the radiation to her brain tumor. Oncology specialists said it would take three months for any results from the radiation. The radiation sent her to an extreme basket case, vomiting, not eating, unable to walk or even go to the toilet on her own. Not just myself that flew to help, her friend she'd known since kind school in Perth came over, also her son flew over from London.

All us nurses that had known and worked with Diana came nearly every day. There were about 30 of us girls and a couple of guys kept a constant eye on her. I was staying at her house, as I was so used to being there, on hand 24/7 hrs. for anything she needed. The girls were fantastic, we were all friends and I set up a nurse's station with a notebook, medications and straws and anything she required. The radiation affected her terribly, she was not aware of what was happening or her behavior. Everyone helped by either making meals, doing shopping, showering her and anything she needed, as she wasn't able to do anything, full care and us girls, being nurses for years knew exactly how to care for our fabulous Diana. At one point I used a syringe to give her fluids as she stopped drinking and eating. Every hour there was always someone to try her to feed or give fluids. I ordered some anti-emetics from her doctor, to help her with the nausea and vomiting. Another one of the girls collected from the chemist. Of course when I refer to us 'girls' most of us were over 60. There were a few younger but still working. Her coworkers were absolutely marvelous, Man deep was Indian and made some incredible soups and dishes for her. Honestly everyone was doing their best for Diana. There were some funny moments that when she got better we told her about and it was hilarious. She needed a shower and a bed change, so two people were on that duty, three people were on bath duty physically caring this screaming lady, yelling

"Help I am being kidnapped! Help they are trying to drown me. You bitch!" She laughed when we told her.

She had no recollection of her birthday despite friends popped in with gifts and words of kindness and love for her. It took her a few days before she was lucid enough to sit up and started drinking with a straw at first then upgraded to a drink bottle. She enjoyed her little cup and saucer for cups of tea. She actually became too well and was demanding her cup be filled with hot water before putting teabag in it, empting that cup and refilling with more hot water. It was quite funny at first, after a while I felt like I was in an episode of The Crown, as scullery maid. Hazel had to send visitors away on days Diana was unwell and incoherent. It was so sad. Three days of hell. Eventually she began to be more focused and began eating and drinking. She seemed hungry a lot, eating well then she would have only half. But that was fine as long she was eating something. With no pressure on her with dealing with work, students, exam marking and definitely no need to constantly watch over Daniel who had been continually drinking himself to obliteration, he had his own Demons. It all was so sad and harder to believe that this shit really happened and the reality is extremely overwhelming. Diana realized that all her friends loved her so much and wished her well. Always by her side and in their hearts. I know she was always in mine.

It's Monday 4th March and waking up in Old with Diana on my mind, wondering how she is coping mentally, emotionally and physically. She tells me she is not in pain, which is a relief to me. Oncology nurses are the best at keeping their patients pain free as much as possible. I did Oncology for many years as I have mentioned previously. She rests in her hospital bed keeping energy for whatever comes next. I love you so much. Saturday 9th March having a peaceful night without any bad dreams as I have endured the last few nights. I had a dream that I was working a night shift in oncology, patients were moaning and groaning sitting upright in their beds with arms outstretched. They gestured for me to help them, I tried not to look at them directly in their faces as it was difficult to look at their distorted bodies. The expressions of unrelenting pain and I was not able to escape into the Treatment room. As I went to open the door, I felt the grip of a bony hand! I woke to discover it was a bad dream. Beads of perspiration gathering under my chin. A breath of relief escaped from my lungs. I crept into my bathroom and washed my face with splashes of cold water. Wondering what caused that nightmarish dream? It was a bittersweet day as my son and his family were inspecting a beautiful 'Hamptons Type home only a few streets away from the waterfront Apartment with its lapping of water on the marina. The two story Hamptons house was so beautiful. It had only been a week since seeing her last.

Oddly enough I was feeling some sort of anticipation from news from the Cancer center, as Diana had received her first dose of radiation and waiting for the Treatment plan. It was 11th April and Hazel was taking her for the Chemotherapy plan for the Stage 4 NSC Lung cancer. Diana lives in hope, we thought at first was denial but it was 'hope' in the truest sense of the word. This terrible diagnosis is not just wrecking her body, but the prognosis is life limiting. We are with her 24 hours a day, every day that she needs us. Despite being the miss independent fabulous Diana that we knew and loved. We needed to respect her wishes. Everyone flocked from London, Perth Queensland. Sadly, she had metastasis in other areas in her body. Treatment is now for quality of life rather than quantity. As an experienced nurse I knew what this meant. Amongst all this her partner had died and was cremated, two weeks post her diagnosis. It was heartbreaking for all of the girls, we could only imagine the devastation Diana must have felt. We were sitting out in her courtyard just us two of us, relaxing having a cuppa, she was having a 'good' day. The Crematorium man rang her to say Daniel's remains were ready. Oh Lord how much could she bear? She requested they deliver them on another day as she couldn't cope. They were fantastic and very understanding. Diana chose another day. From that day on everyone began showering her with practical items such as, a commode chair, shower chair, installing ramps for easy and safe access in and out the front door, into kitchen area, and bedroom, and lounge. Eventually with Ian's genius know-how, transformed her bathroom which had a beautiful bath with lion legs into a fully functional shower with hand rails, toilet raiser the whole area safe to use. All plumbing and electrical repairs were completed, even installed a new dishwasher and fixed the air conditioning in the lounge.

She was improving with using her wheelie walker and sometimes too good. She was a nightmare going to Coles or Woolworths, and we told her so too! The solution being she rests at home with one of the girls and I would go do the shopping. One particular time when I was at Coles or somewhere she rang to ask where to lamb chop dish went from the night before. Oh hell, I had thrown it out as she would only have half of her meals, wrap it put it in fridge and forget it was there. Guess who had to clean the fridge and throw out the day-old dinners. I admitted to her I had disposed of it. My God you would think I had stolen the actual ten commandments off Moses! Eventually she calmed down and forgave me… phew! We had lots of funny days like that. One of her mates Steve, Diana, and I went out in her car, with Steve driving, an ex-cop. Diana was insisting going to a car wash. No worries, Steve pulled into the self-serve bay to wash the car,

"No not that one the other one, automatic one." She was screaming at him at that started a series of unfortunate events that we all later laughed about. Steve steered into the automatic wash over the wheel thingy, water started gushing over the car, Steve was ok until the suds started. He wound down his window enough to stick his head out to breathe. As he put his window up, mainly because Diana was having a fit, I was winding my window down too. Apparently both Steve and I suffer claustrophobia very badly, so here we were having a panic attack and Diana being the only sensible one. OMG it was hilarious, we drove out of the wash bay and sat for ten minutes.

"What the hell is the matter with you two?" she was furious, but after we explained we had a good laugh. She had fun telling the others the story, even to my son Michael.

Back in Old for a few weeks and the others taking turns to stay with her until my next visit early August. I ordered my new Hamptons Style white bed and new Euro mattress and sent Diana photos of my new room. I started writing to her every week to cheer her up. Quite often she would ring me at night and tell me what she had done or who she had seen. It was fantastic to hear her. She loved getting my cheery and funny letters. It was my youngest son's 40th Birthday and Diana wanted to ring him as she had known him since he was 9 years old and living in the Lodge. I was broken-hearted when I got a call on 21st May saying Diana had pneumonia and was in Flinders again. She needed oxygen 24/7. She was admitted to the ICU for 2 days then her Oncology team took over her care in the Respiratory Unit. So pleased she had the best nurses and top specialists. Selfishly I prayed

"Please God don't take her today, my dad passed away today in the same hospital, at 10am I got the call that he had passed, I just couldn't believe it. The void in my life back then created a crater in my heart. Diana had been there for me and helped with that void. What do I do when she leaves this earth? I was feeling very overwhelmed at the moment I just couldn't sit still. My youngest son had driven to Victoria to spend some time with his daughter, Caroline, for her birthday the next day, 22nd May. Please Lord don't take Diana tomorrow either, it's Caroline's birthday. My flight was booked for the 25th May to return to Adelaide to see Diana. 'Please hold on I am on my way over, be with you soon, My fabulous friend Diana.' Feeling of resentment were rising within me, like Daniel, RIP, who wasted her last 2 years and Wayne wasted the last 5 years of my life and yet he lives. Where is the justice in that? Where does it explain in the Bible? My nana was a good woman, Christian as well who loved me as much as I loved her. The Lord took her at 69 years of age. I will be 69 years this year. I am determined to live a long healthy life. My mum lived until 82 years of age. I truly miss them all.

Heal the sick or prolong the process? Arrived back in Adelaide safely and the flight was smooth. I had downloaded a couple of movies on my IPAD which was great as it makes the trip quicker. From the airport I went straight to the Flinders hospital to see Diana, I had to mask up and down the PPE gown etc. Diana was so happy to see me despite her being on a nebulizer I could see her smiling and her brown eyes lit up. There were signs on her curtains 'NO CONTACT, PPE IN USE' Please see nurse. ok I thought owning up with the PPE at end of bed. Have been used to this all my nursing career. When I saw the smile I didn't care I hugged her and for that moment she was my fabulous friend Diana, happy and pain free. Apart from her IVABs and nebulizers, 2 steroids and continuous oxygen via nasal prongs, she was great.! I got the bus to her place and settled in, fed the cat. She was improved enough that they let her come home on the Monday. I drove her car in a collected her. She just couldn't wait to get home to her little sanctuary. We enjoyed a quiet but blissful night together. A few laughs and early to bed. Apparently she slept well, no interruptions from nursing staff, other patients ringing the buzzers or IV machines beeping. She was home in every sense of the word. It was amazing to watch her ambulating around the house with her walker. Independent to bathroom, bedroom, kitchen and her favourite place the courtyard.

Hazel, Pauline, Mandy, Jill, Louise, and Kathy from Perth all visited her and she absolutely had a wonderful time enjoying quality time with all her friends. The last time we were all together she was too unwell to remember any of it. So we made it up to her. Dinner parties and set the dining table like the Queen was invited, take-away Indian Cuisine, breakfasts at Becks Bakery. Anything she wanted. Eventually, she was able to go through all her birthday gifts. There were also some Sympathy cards for the loss of Daniel. She cried after everyone left and it was just us. Diana only wanted to remember the positive aspects of Daniel not the last two years of hell. That was ok too. That is how she could cope and it was her life to be as happy as she could. We watched movies on Netflix, we would be in absolute stitches laughing. We all made her last months be full of love. Her sons were beside her, but it was really difficult for them to grieve in front of her, so keeping it all inside created a strain on the inside, and it was harder to talk about it to each other. She found it hard to talk to them about her cancer and made it clear she didn't want to be treated as a 'cancer patient' to define her. She wanted to survive this and return to work. Every now and then a few of us girls would open the discussion on Palliative Care nurses to check on her now and then if one of us wasn't available. It was a touchy subject and caused a bit of tension with Diana. She felt that Palliative Care was 'end of life' it is sad for those who need it are scared to use it. I feel this needs more positive awareness to make the stigma less scary for patients with limited life expectancy.

By the 13th of June I was back in QLD, moving into the big house with my eldest son and his wife, Sonya and granddaughter. Diana was so excited to see me settled and happy. I wrote every week. Pathology was due every 3rd week, so the results would be received by her Oncologist prior to her treatment. One time I took her there, with Kathy in toe, hoping to talk to the Oncologist on her situation. She never allowed anyone in, that was not our normal Diana... keeping secrets like that or not being frank about something. The situation must be really scary if she couldn't tell any of girls. It was like we knew but no one was saying it out loud. Diana finally agreed to get her 'affairs' in order. One of the girls helped her with that. Unfortunately a couple of times she cancelled appointments to finalize the documents with the lawyer. We had to be firm with her. Hazel was the one who would tell her straight. Luckily I was there when the lawyer came, so she had no choice by to sign them and get even her End of Life preferences documented. We had discussed it but she had to write it. Say it out loud. I found this was one of the hardest part of watching your loved one going through something like this and decide when enough is enough. Her brother was made Executive of the Willi flew back to QLD and planned to come back early August.

Diana and I were continuing to have chats on the phone although she was rushed and said she was tired and going to bed. That was ok. Then I get quick calls saying her incontinence is improving as she not voiding at night. This sent an alarm bell off in my nursing head. She was increasingly tired, reduction in voiding and treatment not needed now, she had 'improved'. I was concerned about her and kept in touch with the other girls as Hazel and her hubby were going on their annual 3 monthly trek around Australia. Deep down I fear she was going to miss Hazel and panic, but would not allow us to get the Palliative Care and Oncology nurses to help in the home or personal care. She was miss independent Diana! On Thursday 25th July she had her 3 monthly review with the Radiologist at Dew Park. He was not going to continue any further treatment. There was nothing else to do. She told everyone that she was improving and didn't need any further radiation. The sad but truth was the Radiologist and the Oncologists informed her that the Radiation was not successful, in fact the tumor had increased in size and the MRI revealed two more tumors on her other lung. The cancer had metastasized to other areas of her body and another in the brain. She only told one person in confidence, and it wasn't one of us nurses.

On Friday 26th July Diana managed to get one of her workmates to take her to work just so she could see her students. She wanted to have a normal day. She apparently sat in a wheelchair and observed the class. At midday, she walked with the walking frame to the nearby shopping center, did some shopping, and called an Uber. We think she was at the wrong meeting place. She then rang another Uber but that didn't show up either. I believe a third Uber was called and she got home late in the afternoon. She had dinner and a movie at home with Mandy, another nurse mate, Diana told her,

"Marsha is coming over to see me this week!" she was very excited according to Mandy. And we chatted on the phone about it on Thursday night. Mandy left her after the movie and was going to pop in on Saturday or Sunday. In any case the worse happened. I checked flights to Adelaide, I sent her a few text messages but no reply. Okay, she must have some friends over, try her later. I received a message from one of the girls, apparently Diana had fallen on the laundry floor, a meter or so away from where Daniel had fallen. She had been on the floor for over 30 hours up to 48 hours! The ambulance was called instantly by the girls who found her. Rushed to Emergency and straight into ICU. Her brother was called, I txt Diana to say I knew she was in hospital and was on my way to her. This was Monday 29th July. I received the call from her brother at 7.20am Tuesday 30th July, stating 'she's gone'.

My heart stopped for a second. I cried and sent my condolences to her and her two sons. She loved both those boys. I don't recall what happened next. I was devastated beyond words. All of us girls felt a tremendous loss. I had lost my fabulous friend Diana. There are no words. 30th July 2024. Will remember that date for the rest of my life. My loving son bought me some beautiful flowers after work that day. They were amazing and so thoughtful of him. I contacted my youngest son as he had known her as long as I had and knew her sons when they were all about 9 and 10 years old. He loved her too. I didn't know what to feel, how to feel. Grief for my loss or relief for her, pain-free and flying high with her Daniel. I knew I would miss her terribly. I cried so hard I fell asleep from the darkness in my heart. Please Diana send me some butterflies.